2000 MOST COMMON FRENCH WORDS IN CONTEXT

Get Fluent & Increase Your French Vocabulary with 2000 French Phrases

French Language Lessons

ISBN-13:978-1724979230

FREE BOOK REVEALS THE 6 STEP BLUEPRINT THAT TOOK STUDENTS **FROM LANGUAGE LEARNERS TO FLUENT IN 3 MONTHS**

- **6 Unbelievable Hacks** that will accelerate your learning curve
- **Mind Training:** why memorizing vocabulary is easy
- **One Hack To Rule Them All:** This secret nugget will blow you away...

Head over to LingoMastery.com/hacks
and claim your free book now!

INTRODUCTION

Just like any other goal you set for yourself in life, learning a new language can be intimidating at first and may seem like a mountain to climb. You'll spend a lot of time talking or thinking about it, but actually *doing* something about it? Easier said than done. Learning a language is just like dieting, really: it's easy to postpone and it takes a lot of motivation to get started, but when you finally get into it and start to see results as you go along, you'll find that it is extremely rewarding, in so many ways.

Indeed, knowing more than one language isn't just something to brag about. It's a valuable asset to your overall knowledge, and it gives you an in depth and personal access to a whole new culture: music, literature, history, science, sociology, gastronomy... and most importantly, you will get the unique chance to discuss, share and learn with remarkable people you would otherwise never have met.

When you face yourself in the mirror and finally decide to go on a diet, it's because you have an objective in mind – a final goal – which will take time to achieve. The same goes with learning a new language: your objective, reason or purpose will help you stay focused and motivated along the way, no matter how long it takes. It's true: *every* learner is different, has his or her own ways and progresses at his or her own pace. Setting unreasonable goals for yourself or trying to rush into things will definitely affect your level of interest, which is why you need to constantly remind yourself of your objectives, keep track of your progress and make sure you're doing it for the right reasons. In the end, learning a new language will help you learn more about yourself.

When you ask yourself the question "Why should I learn to speak French?", consider this:

French is one of the few languages that is spoken and taught on all five continents, with over 220 million speakers worldwide. It is ranked the sixth most widely spoken language in the world and is the official language for 29 countries, which puts it right after English in this category. Being able to communicate fluently in French will not only give you access to more leisure travel destinations, it will also allow you to become a valuable candidate for quality job opportunities around the globe: many large companies – and that's a fact – will favor a bilingual candidate, since they have the capacity to communicate with a larger amount of existing or potential clients and can be understood on a much larger territory.

If you picked up this book and are still reading at this point, the hardest part – actually *doing* something about it – is already behind you and you're on your way to become a French speaker yourself. This book can give you a very useful tool in learning the French language: *vocabulary.* Now all that's left to learn is how to use it.

What this book is about and how to use it:

Being a French teacher, I am very well aware that learning the language can rapidly become overwhelming when you think of the numerous aspects of grammar, punctuation rules, syntax and coherence, and I won't even get started on all the exceptions inherent to the French language... but don't be alarmed: even my native French student have a hard time getting to learn all the aspects of their mother tongue. French is a beautiful language, but it is also a tricky one. That said, what's the best way to get started? What does every new learner *really* want when tackling a new language, officially or unofficially? The answer is simple:

They want to expand their vocabulary.

And that's exactly where you'll want to start. Indeed, when learning a new tongue, becoming familiar with the vocabulary is the most effective way to speed up the process. Just look at these three impressive statistics found in a study done in 1964:

1. *Learning the first thousand (1000) most frequently used words of a language will allow you to understand 76.0% of all non-fiction writing, 79.6% of all fiction writing and an astounding 87.8% of all oral speech.*

2. *Learning the top two thousand (2000) most frequently used words will get you to 84% for non-fiction, 86.1% for fiction, and 92.7% for oral speech.*

3. *Learning the top three thousand (3000) most frequently used words will get you to 88.2% for non-fiction, 89.6% for fiction, and 94.0% for oral speech.*

This book will provide you with the top two thousand most frequently used words in the French language, equivalent to an understanding of 92.7% of oral speech according to these statistics. Just think of all the things you'll be able to achieve thanks to this book and a little practice!

But to get to this point, an ordinary list of 2000 terms won't be of much help. This is why we provide you with words that are in context, carefully placed in a sentence where they can express their true meaning. Each term will be listed alongside its translation (or translations, when applicable) in English, along with two example sentences (one in each language), for a deeper understanding of the term. This method will make the vocabulary more accessible to you, since you can compare it to English words that are also in context for reference. The terms have been selected according to their occurrences in a corpus of various media containing more than 20 million words of text and speech from all around the world – not just from a specific pool of French speakers. To make this vocabulary lesson more significant to you, we have ordered all 2000 terms of this book according to their frequency of use in said media.

After reading this book, you might be tempted to ask: "Is that it?" Well of course, there's always something more to learn. As you know, there are thousands and thousands of words in the French language, but the 2000 we provide you with will certainly give you a head-start on learning the language and help you in getting closer to mastering it.

Recommendations for readers of *2000 Most Common Words in French:*

Although we'd love to begin right away with helping you learn the vocabulary we've provided in this book, we've got a few tips and recommendations for getting the most out of your lesson:

1. An example you read can be transformed into an example you write. Why not try to practice the words we provide you by using them in your own sentences? If you can master this, you will not only be practicing your vocabulary, but also the use of verbs, nouns and sentences in general.
2. Why limit yourself to 2000 words? While you're reading this book, you can always find 2000 more *not-so-frequently-used* words and practice them as well!
3. Grab a partner or two and practice with them. Maybe it's your boyfriend/girlfriend, your roomie or even your parents; learning in groups is always easier than learning alone, and you can find somebody to practice your oral speech with. Just make sure they practice as hard as you do, since you don't want a lazy team-mate here!
4. Use the vocabulary you've learned to write a story and share it with others to see how good (or bad) it is! Find help from a native speaker and let them help you improve.

IMPORTANT NOTE: Many words in French are inherently *masculine* or *feminine*. These words include most nouns, which are generally preceded by their concordant determinant: **Le/Un** for masculine and **La/Une** for feminine. Other words are what we could call "gender neutral", as they can be applied to both genders while keeping the same orthograph. This is the case for many pronouns. Also, just to complicate things further, the masculine prevails over the feminine in most collective nouns or expressions, meaning they *must* take the masculine form when they include at least one masculine subject within them (for example: **Chanteurs -** *Singers*, where at least one male must be present unless you mean to write **Chanteuses** for an all-women group). This might seem like a lot to take in but don't worry, I've got you covered: when a word's gender is variable, I've always included both the masculine and feminine forms to save you the hassle. In French, every sentence needs a subject and every subject has a gender, so make sure to take this into account when you use the words in the future, because choosing the wrong form can highly affect your sentence! For example, we can all agree that it would be silly for a man to call himself a **Mécanicienne** – *Mechanic (Feminine)*, or for a woman to say that she's a **Coiffeur** – *Hairdresser (Masculine)*!

One last thing before we start. If you haven't already, head over to <u>LingoMastery.com/hacks</u> and grab a copy of our free Lingo Hacks book that will teach you the important secrets that you need to know to become fluent in a language as fast as possible. Again, you can find the free book over at <u>LingoMastery.com/hacks</u>.

Now, without further ado, we can finally get started on our lesson! Have fun learning French, beloved reader!

Good luck!

THE 2000 MOST COMMON WORDS IN FRENCH

Here we are. As I previously stated in the **Introduction,** the words have been arranged by their frequency of use according to a corpus of various French media, written or spoken, such as any form of literature, films and series. Feel free to rearrange them during your practice to make things interesting! Also, you'll find that some words are repeated from one phrase to the other (inevitably), so make sure to take notes or use the search function if you own the digital version of this book to compare the different occurrences!

You will be provided with a **French word**, an **English translation of said word** and **two examples** (one in each language) for the given term. French words that vary according to the gender will always be presented in the following order: masculine|feminine. It's as simple as that!

Now, let us begin:

1- Un|Une – *A/An/One*

J'ai vu **une** femme à l'hôpital; **un** de ses bras était cassé.
I saw **a** woman at the hospital; **one** of her arms was broken.

2- À – *To*

Je vais **à** Paris avec mes parents et ma petite soeur cet été.
I am going **to** Paris with my parents and my little sister this summer.

3- En – *In/By*

L'an prochain, je serai **en** Irlande. J'irai **en** train.
Next year, I will be **in** Ireland. I will go **by** train.

4- Le|La – *The*

Je veux adopter **le** chat et **la** lapine que nous avons vus au refuge.
I want to adopt **the** cat and **the** bunny that we saw at the shelter.

5- Et – *And*

Nous sommes faits pour être ensemble, toi **et** moi.
We are made for each other, you **and** I.

6- Être – *To be*

Pas besoin d'**être** un champion du monde pour s'amuser au golf.
No need **to be** a world champion to enjoy yourself while playing golf.

7- De – *From*

La grand-mère de mon père venait **de** Pologne.
My father's grandmother was **from** Poland.

8- Avoir – *To have*

Il est difficile d'**avoir** du temps pour soi quand on travaille trop.
It is difficult **to have** time for yourself when you work too much.

9- Que – *That/Who/Whom*

La jeune fille **que** j'ai rencontrée hier était enseignante.
The young lady **whom** I met yesterday was a school teacher.

10- Ne – *Not*

Je **ne** crois pas que tu aies fait le bon choix.
I do **not** believe you made the right choice.

11- Dans – *In/Into*

J'ai mis une bouteille d'eau **dans** ton sac à dos.
I put a water bottle **in** your backpack.

12- Ce|Cette – *This/That*

Ce nouveau magasin vient d'ouvrir de l'autre côté de la rue.
This new shop just opened across the street.

13- Il – *He/It*

Il m'a dit qu'**il** était déjà huit heures.
He told me **it** was already eight o'clock.

14- Qui – *Who/Whom*

Qui a mangé la dernière part de gâteau?
Who ate the last piece of cake?

15- Pas – *Not/-n't*

Le concert commence à dix-neuf heures, ne sois **pas** en retard.
The show starts at seven o'clock, do**n't** be late.

16- Pour – *For*

J'ai acheté un bouquet de roses **pour** ma mère, ce sont ses fleurs preferés.
I bought a bouquet of roses **for** my mother, they are her favorite flowers.

17- Sur – *On*

Pose les assiettes **sur** la table et assieds-toi.
Put the plates **on** the table and take a seat.

18- Se – *Himself/Herself/Themselves*

S'il continue à être aussi imprudent, il va **se** blesser.
If he keeps being so careless, he is going to hurt **himself**.

19- Son – *His/Her/Its*

Elle a invité **son** mari au restaurant pour la St-Valentin.
She invited **her** husband to the restaurant for Valentine's Day.

20- Plus – *More/No more*

Jacques voudrait **plus** de salade de fruit, mais il n'en reste **plus**.
Jacques would want **more** fruit salad, but there is **no more** left.

21- Pouvoir – *Can/To be able to*

Le fait de **pouvoir** dormir tard le dimanche matin me rend heureux.
The fact that I **can** sleep late on Sunday morning makes me happy.

22- Par – *By*

Connais-tu la chanson *Une Colombe* **par** Céline Dion?
Do you know the song *Une Colombe* **by** Céline Dion?

23- Je – *I*

Je crois que ma mère est la femme la plus respectable au monde.
I think that my mother is the most respectable woman in the world.

24- Avec – *With*

Je suis trop timide pour lui demander d'aller au cinéma **avec** moi.
I am too shy to ask her to go to the movies **with** me.

25- Tout – *All*

J'ai reçu **tout** ce que je voulais pour mon anniversaire.
I received **all** that I wanted for my birthday.

26- Faire – *To do/To make*

Pierre ne **fait** jamais à dîner, je dois tout **faire** moi-même.
Pierre never **makes** dinner, I must **do** everything myself.

27- Nous – *We/Us*

Nous croyons que tu devrais **nous** accompagner à la fête ce soir.
We think that you should accompany **us** to the party tonight.

28- Mettre – *To put*

Va **mettre** ton assiette dans le lave-vaisselle quand tu as fini.
Go **put** your plate in the dishwasher when you're done.

29- Autre – *Other*

Sa voiture ne fonctionne plus, elle doit en acheter une **autre**.
Her car no longer works, she needs to buy an**other**.

30- On – *We/One*

On va tous chez Sara! **On** pourrait dire qu'elle sait faire la fête!
We're all going to Sara's! **One** might say that she knows how to party!

31- Mais – *But*

Elle était réellement une femme forte, **mais** elle était si fatiguée.
She really was a strong woman, **but** she was so tired.

32- Leur – *Their*

Cette troupe de théâtre est incroyable, as-tu vu **leur** dernière pièce?
This theater troupe is incredible, have you seen **their** latest play?

33- Comme – *Like*

Lorsque je serai grande, je ne veux pas être **comme** ma mère.
When I get older, I don't want to be **like** my mother.

34- Ou – *Or*

Quelle saveur préfères-tu : chocolat **ou** vanille?
Which flavor do you prefer: chocolate **or** vanilla?

35- Si – *If*

Si j'étais riche, j'aurais déménagé dans le Sud de la France depuis longtemps.
If I was rich, I would have moved to the south of France long ago.

36- Avant – *Before*

Embrasse-moi **avant** de partir; tu vas me manquer.
Kiss me **before** you leave; I'm going to miss you.

37- Y – *There*

Paris a l'air magnifique, j'ai vraiment envie d'**y** aller.
Paris seems wonderful, I really want to go **there**.

38- Dire – *To say*

Il y a tellement de choses que j'ai envie de te **dire** avant que tu partes.
There are so many things I want **to say** to you before you leave.

39- Elle – *She/Her*

Elle est malade. Son père prendra soin d'**elle**.
She is sick. Her father will take care of **her**.

40- Devoir – To have to/To owe

Tu lui **dois** trois cents dollars! Tu **dois** absolument le rembourser.
You **owe** him three hundred dollars! You absolutely **have to** repay him.

41- Donner – *To give*

Je n'utilise jamais mon four micro-ondes, alors je vais te le **donner**.
I never use my microwave, so I'll **give** it to you.

42- Deux – *Two*

Il est difficile de trouver un nouvel appartement quand on a **deux** chiens.

It's hard to find a new apartment when one has **two** dogs.

43- Même – *Same/Even*

Karine a acheté la **même** robe, **même** si je lui avais dit de ne pas le faire.

Karine bought the **same** dress, **even** though I had told her not to.

44- Prendre – *To take*

N'oublie pas de **prendre** tes clés avant de partir.

Don't forget **to take** your keys before you go.

45- Où – *Where*

Où vas-tu? Reviens ici tout de suite!

Where are you going? Come back here this instant!

46- Aussi – *Also/As ... as*

Je crois que Marine est **aussi** belle que l'aurore. Le crois-tu **aussi**?

I think that Marine is **as** beautiful **as** the dawn. Do you **also** think that?

47- Celui|Celle – *The one*

Tu vois l'homme dans le coin là-bas? C'est **celui** dont je t'ai parlé.

See the man in the corner over there? That's **the one** I told you about.

48- Bien – *Well*

J'ai entendu dire que Maxime ne se sentait pas **bien** aujourd'hui.

I heard that Maxime was not feeling **well** today.

49- Cela – *That*

De quoi parles-tu? **Cela** n'a aucun sens!
What are you talking about? **That** makes no sense!

50- Vous – *You (formal)*

Vous êtes la raison que je suis venue ici ce soir, madame.
You are the reason why I came here tonight, madam.

51- Encore – *Again/Yet*

Oh non, pas **encore**! Nous ne sommes même pas **encore** partis!
Oh no, not **again**! We didn't even leave **yet**!

52- Vouloir – *To want*

Il est normal de **vouloir** être aimé.
It is normal **to want** to be loved.

53- Nouveau|Nouvelle – *New*

J'ai besoin d'une **nouvelle** chemise pour le mariage de ma soeur.
I need a **new** shirt for my sister's wedding.

54- Aller – *To go*

Je t'amènerais jusqu'au bout du monde. Où veux-tu **aller**?
I would take you to the end of the world. Where do you want **to go**?

55- Entre – *Between*

Il n'y a plus de magie **entre** nous.
There is no more magic **between** us.

56- Premier|Première – *First*

La compétition s'est très bien déroulée : Philippe a terminé **premier**.
The competition went really well: Philippe finished **first**.

57- Aucun|Aucune – *None/No*

Il n'y a **aucune** voyelle dans mon nom. C'est vrai! Il n'y en a **aucune**.

There is **no** vowel in my name. It's true! There is **none**.

58- Déjà – **Already**

Pardon, je ne savais pas que tu étais **déjà** là.

Sorry, I didn't know you were **already** here.

59- Grand|Grande – *Tall*

Je ne peux pas sortir avec cette fille, elle est beaucoup trop **grande**!

I can't go out with this girl, she is way too **tall**!

60- Mon|Ma – *My*

Je déteste laisser **mon** chien seul à la maison.

I hate to leave **my** dog alone at home.

61- Me – *Myself*

Je dois être prudent avec ce couteau, j'ai failli **me** blesser la dernière fois!

I must be careful with that knife, I almost hurt **myself** last time!

62- Moins – *Less*

Ce serait bon pour ta santé si tu essayais de manger **moins** gras.

It would be good for your health if you tried to eat **less** fat.

63- Quelques – *Some*

J'ai ramené deux pommes et **quelques** abricots de l'épicerie.

I brought back two apples and **some** apricots from the grocery store.

64- Lui – *Him/Her*

Il **lui** a demandé d'aller au bal avec **lui**, mais elle a dit non!
He asked **her** to go to the ball with **him**, but she said no!

65- Un temps – *A time*

Il fut **un temps** où l'essence coûtait moins d'un dollar le litre.
There was **a time** when gas cost less than one dollar per litre.

66- Très – *Very*

Le gâteau à la vanille de ta mère est **très** bon.
Your mother's vanilla cake is **very** good.

67- Savoir – *To know*

Il est important de **savoir** cuisiner lorsqu'on habite seul.
It's important **to know** how to cook when you live alone.

68- Falloir – *To need/To require*

Il va **falloir** que tu remettes ce devoir avant mercredi.
You will **need** to hand in this homework before Wednesday.

69- Voir – *To see*

Le soleil brillait si fort qu'elle n'arrivait pas à **voir** la route.
The sun was shining so bright that she could not **see** the road.

70- Notre – *Our*

Nous avons finalement réussi à vendre **notre** maison.
We have finally managed to sell **our** house.

71- Sans – *Without*

Dites ce que vous voulez, mais je préfère manger mes céréales **sans** lait.
Say what you will, but I prefer to eat my cereal **without** milk.

72- Dont – *Whose/Of which*

Le voisin **dont** la femme est décédée l'an dernier vient de déménager.
The neighbor **whose** wife died last year just moved away.

73- Une raison – *A reason*

Donne-moi **une raison** de ne pas te jeter dehors!
Give me **a reason** not to kick you out!

74- Le monde – *The world/People*

Nous vivons dans **un monde** où **le monde** est trop centré sur lui-même.
We live in a **world** where **people** are too self-centered.

75- Non – *No/Not/Non-*

Non! J'ai demandé de l'eau et **non** du soda! **Non** gazéuse!
No! I asked for water, **not** soda! **Non-**carbonated!

76- Monsieur – *Mister/Sir*

Monsieur, je crois que vous n'avez pas encore payé l'addition.
Sir, I believe you haven't paid the bill yet.

77- Un an – *A year*

Ça fait déjà **un an** que j'ai vu ma cousine Sophie.
It's already been **a year** since I've last seen my cousin Sophie.

78- Un jour – *One day*

Un jour, j'étudierai dans une université réputée.
One day, I will study in a reputable university.

79- Trouver – *To find*

J'ai cherché partout mais je n'arrive pas à **trouver** mes clés!
I looked everywhere but I can't seem **to find** my keys!

80- Demander – *To ask*

Je ne sais pas, va **demander** à ta mère!
I don't know, go **ask** your mother!

81- Alors – *Then*

Le voyage est annulé? Qu'est-ce qu'on va faire, **alors**?
The trip is cancelled? What are we going to do, **then**?

82- Après – *After*

Je dois aller chercher ma petite soeur **après** l'école.
I have to go pick up my sister **after** school.

83- Venir – *To come*

Sylvie a une intoxication alimentaire, elle ne pourra pas **venir** avec nous.
Sylvie has food poisoning, she won't be able **to come** with us.

84- Une personne – *A person*

Je connais **une personne** qui peut chanter l'opéra merveilleusement.
I know **a person** who can sing opera beautifully.

85- Rendre – *To give back*

Gérard, tu dois lui **rendre** son téléphone portable avant qu'il se fâche.
Gérard, you have **to give** him his cellphone **back** before he gets angry.

86- Une part – *A share*

J'ai acheté **une part** de cette entreprise.
I bought **a share** of this company.

17

87- Dernier|Dernière – *Last*

La **dernière** chose que je veux, c'est de te voir souffrir.
The **last** thing I want is to see you suffer.

88- Lequel|Laquelle – *Which (one)*

Lequel de ces sports préfères-tu? Le hockey ou le football?
Which one of these sports do you prefer? Hockey or football?

89- Pendant – *During*

Carl était en Floride **pendant** l'été.
Carl was in Florida **during** the summer.

90- Passer – *To pass*

Essaie de **passer** la balle parfois, c'est un sport d'équipe!
Try **to pass** the ball sometimes, it's a team sport!

91- Un peu – *A little*

J'aimerais avoir juste **un peu** de ketchup avec mes frites, s'il-vous-plaît.
I'd like to have just **a little** ketchup with my fries, please.

92- Depuis – *Since/For*

Nous sommes mariés **depuis** vingt ans.
We have been married **for** twenty years.

93- La suite – *What follows*

J'ai hâte au prochain épisode, j'aimerais connaître **la suite**.
I can't wait for the next episode, I'd like to know **what follows**.

94- Bon|Bonne – *Good*

Merci Mireille, le repas que tu as préparé ce soir était très **bon**.
Thank you, Mireille, the meal that you prepared this evening was very **good**.

95- Comprendre – *To understand*

Je te l'ai déjà dit vingt fois, quand vas-tu **comprendre**?
I told you twenty times already, when will you **understand**?

96- Rester – *To stay*

Tu dois **rester**, la fête vient tout juste de commencer!
You must **stay**, the party has only just begun!

97- Un point – *A point*

Il a mis de l'avant **un point** très intéressant lors de son exposé.
He has brought forward a very interesting **point** during his presentation.

98- Ainsi – *Thus*

Il est **ainsi** très important de suivre les instructions à la lettre.
It is **thus** very important to follow the instructions to the letter.

99- Une heure – *An hour*

Je t'attends au parc depuis **une heure**.
I have been waiting for you at the park for **an hour**.

100- Une année – *A year*

Depuis combien d'**années** habitez-vous ici?
How many **years** have you lived here?

101- Toujours – *Always*

Je serai **toujours** là pour toi, peu importe ce qui se passe.
I will **always** be there for you, no matter what happens.

102- Tenir – *To hold*

N'oublis pas de **tenir** la main de ton frère avant de traverser la rue.
Don't forget **to hold** your brother's hand before you cross the street.

103- Porter – *To wear/To carry*

Tu veux **porter** des talons hauts? Tu auras mal aux pieds et je devrai encore te **porter** sur mes épaules!
You want **to wear** high heels? Your feet will hurt and I'll have **to carry** you on my shoulders again!

104- Parler – *To speak/To talk (to)*

J'ai vraiment besoin de **parler** à quelqu'un à.
I really need someone **to talk to**.

105- Seul|Seule – *Alone*

Ma meilleure amie ne peut pas venir, alors j'irai **seule**.
My best friend can't come, so I'll go **alone**.

106- Montrer – *To show*

Viens par ici, j'ai quelque chose à te **montrer**!
Come over here, I have something **to show** you!

107- Là – *There*

J'ai entendu un bruit étrange… Qui va **là**?
I heard a stange noise… Who goes **there**?

108- Certain|Certaine – *Certain/Sure*

Joannie, es-tu **certaine** de vouloir acheter cette voiture?
Joannie, are you **sure** you want to buy that car?

109- Fort – *Strong*

Je n'aime pas ce vin, il est trop **fort**.
I do not like this wine, it is too **strong**.

110- Tu – *You (Informal)*

Tu aimes les chats et j'aime les chiens, ça ne pourra jamais fonctionner.
You like cats and I like dogs, it can never work out.

111- Continuer – *To continue*

J'aimerais **continuer** cette conversation une autre fois.
I would like **to continue** this conversation another time.

112- Un pays –*A country*

Le Canada est **un pays** incroyable, rempli de beaux paysages.
Canada is a wonderful **country**, filled with beautiful landscapes.

113- La fin – *The end*

Tu dois absolument payer le loyer avant **la fin** de la semaine.
You absolutely must pay rent before **the end** of the week.

114- Penser – *To think*

Je besoin de temps pour **penser** à ce que nous pourrions faire demain soir.
I need some time **to think** about what we could do tomorrow tonight.

115- Un lieu – *A place*

Le Québec est **un lieu** magnifique et son histoire est captivante.
Quebec is a wonderful **place** and its history is captivating.

116- Une partie – *A part*

La musique est **une partie** importante de ma vie.
Music is an important **part** of my life.

117- Quand – *When*

Quand vas-tu enfin répondre à mes messages?
When will you finally respond to my messages?

118- Trois – *Three*

Je dois partir, mon vol est dans **trois** heures.
I must leave, my flight is in **three** hours.

119- Contre – *Against*

La traversée sera beaucoup plus longue si nous navigons **contre** le vent.
The crossing will be much longer if we sail **against** the wind.

120- Sous – *Under*

Je te rejoindrai **sous** le pont à minuit.
I will meet you **under** the bridge at midnight.

121- Le côté – *The side*

J'ai planté des tomates et des concombres sur **le côté** de la maison.
I have planted tomatoes and cucumbers on **the side** of the house.

122- Ensemble – *Together*

Nous jouons **ensemble** au tennis tous les mercredis.
We play tennis **together** every Wednesday.

123- Une chose – *A thing*

J'ai **une chose** très importante à faire avant de partir.
I have a very important **thing** to do before I leave.

124- Un|Une enfant – *A child*

Ma sœur sait comment s'occuper d'**un enfant**.
My sister knows how to take care of **a child**.

125- Suivre – *To follow*

C'est simple : tu dois **suivre** les instructions.
It's simple: you need **to follow** instructions.

126- Une cause – *A cause*

Il y a **une cause** à toute conséquence.
There is **a cause** to every consequence.

127- Une place – *A space/A place*

Je hais le centre-ville, c'est impossible de trouver **une place** de stationnement.

I hate the city centre, it's impossible to find a parking **space**.

128- Seulement – *Only*

J'ai **seulement** cinquante dollars dans mon compte en banque.

I **only** have fifty dollars in my bank account.

129- Moi – *Me*

Ma mère aime le poisson, mais pas **moi**; je préfère le poulet.

My mother likes fish, but not **me**; I prefer chicken.

130- La vie – *The life*

Grâce à toi, j'ai **la vie** dont j'ai toujours rêvé.

Thanks to you, I have **the life** I've always dreamed of.

131- La politique – *Politics*

J'ai toujours été intéressée par **la politique**.

I've always been interested by **politics**.

132- Jusque/Jusqu' – *To/Until*

On doit se rendre **jusque** chez moi avant huit heures. **Jusqu'**à quelle heure travailles-tu?

We have to get **to** my house before eight o'clock. **Until** what time do you work?

133- Croire – *To believe*

Tu ne dois pas **croire** tout ce tu lis sur l'Internet.

You must not **believe** everything you read on the Internet.

134- Un homme – *A man*

Il y a **un homme** dans le salon.
There's **a man** in the living room.

135- Un cas – *A case*

Dans ce **cas**, je serai à la maison avant neuf heures.
In that **case**, I'll be home before nine.

136- Connaître – *To know*

J'aimerais beaucoup apprendre à te **connaître**.
I would really love to get **to know** you.

137- Commencer – *To begin/To start*

Je vais **commencer** à faire mes valises, je pars demain.
I will **start** packing, I leave tomorrow.

138- Compter – *To count*

Mon neveu de quatre ans a déjà appris à **compter** jusqu'à cent.
My four-year-old nephew has already learned **to count** to a hundred.

139- Un fait – *A fact*

Je l'ai vu dans un documentaire, c'est **un fait**!
I saw it in a documentary, it's **a fact**!

140- Tel|Telle – *Such*

Une **telle** œuvre d'art devrait être affichée dans un musée!
Such a work of art should be exposed in a museum!

141- Petit|Petite – *Small*

Mon chien est **petit**, mais il a beaucoup d'amour à donner.
My dog is **small**, but he has a lot of love to give.

142- Une question – *A question*

Où est Martin? J'ai **une question** à lui poser.
Where is Martin? I have **a question** to ask him.

143- Donc – *So/Therefore*

J'ai manqué l'autobus, **donc** je serai en retard à ton récital.
I missed the bus, **so** I'll be late to your recital.

144- Quel|Quelle – *What/Which*

Quelle est ta saveur de crème glacée favorite?
What is your favorite ice cream flavor?

145- Général|Générale – *General*

J'aime la musique en **général**, peu importe le style.
I love music in **general**, no matter the style.

146- Entendre – *To hear*

Parle plus fort, je ne peux pas t'**entendre** avec tout ce bruit!
Speak louder, I can't **hear** you with all that noise!

147- Beaucoup – *A lot/Many*

Ce film est excellent, **beaucoup** de gens m'en ont parlé.
This movie is excellent, **a lot** of people told me about it.

148- Chaque – *Each/Every*

Chaque personne est différente et tu dois l'accepter.
Every person is different, and you need to accept that.

149- Le droit – *The right*

Maintenant que j'ai dix-huit ans, j'ai **le droit** de voter.
Now that I'm eighteen, I have **the right** to vote.

150- Un moment – *A moment*

La lionne attend le bon **moment** avant d'attaquer sa proie.
The lioness waits for the right **moment** before attacking her prey.

151- Le travail – *Work*

Depuis que son mari est décédé, elle se réfugie dans son **travail**.
Since her husband died, she takes refuge in her **work**.

152- Une femme – *A woman/A wife*

Cette **femme** est extraordinaire. Un jour, j'e la ferai ma **femme**!
This **woman** is amazing. One day, I will make her my **wife**!

153- Attendre – *To wait*

D'accord, je vais t'**attendre** avant de partir, mais fais vite!
Fine, I'll **wait** for you before I leave, but hurry up!

154- Remettre – *To put back*

Je te donne cinq seconds pour **remettre** ton portable dans ta poche.
I give you five seconds **to put** your phone **back** in your pocket.

155- Jeune – *Young*

Je n'arrive pas à croire qu'elle soit déjà diplômée, elle est si **jeune**!
I can't believe she has already graduated, she's so **young**!

156- Permettre – *To allow*

Le gouvernement ne peut pas **permettre** ce genre de choses.
The government can't **allow** these kinds of things.

157- Occupé|Occupée – *Occupied/Busy*

Pardonnez-moi monsieur, ce siège est-il **occupé**?
Pardon me sir, is this seat **occupied**?

158- Le gouvernement – *The government*

Je crois que **le gouvernement** doit honorer ses engagements.
I believe **the government** has to honour its commitments.

159- Eux|Elles – *Them*

J'irai au centre commercial avec **eux** demain.
I will go to the mall with **them** tomorrow.

160- Appeler – *To call*

J'ai entendu un bruit… je vais **appeler** la police!
I heard a noise… I'll **call** the police!

161- Devenir – *To become*

Ce cocon va **devenir** un joli papillon dans quelques jours.
This cocoon will **become** a beautiful butterfly in a couple of days.

162- Partir – *To leave*

Nous allons être en retard, nous devons **partir** maintenant!
We are going to be late, we need **to leave** now!

163- Décider – *To decide*

Il ne reste plus beaucoup de temps, tu dois **décider** pour qui voter.
There isn't much time left, you need **to decide** who to vote for.

164- Soit – *Either... or*

C'est simple : **soit** tu te calmes, **soit** tu marches jusqu'à la maison.
It's simple: **either** you calm down **or** you walk home.

165- Ici – *Here*

Où est Marc? Je croyais qu'il était déjà **ici**.
Where is Marc? I thought he was already **here**.

166- Rien – *Nothing*

Depuis que Jacques est parti, je n'ai plus **rien** à faire ici.
Since Jacques left, I have **nothing** left to do here.

167- Un plan – *A plan*

L'entraîneur a un bon **plan** pour mener l'équipe à la victoire.
The coach has a good **plan** to lead the team to victory.

168- Un cours – *A course*

Elle a pris **un cours** de français pour perfectionner son vocabulaire.
She took a French **course** in order to perfect her vocabulary.

169- Un nom – *A name*

Je croyais qu'elle était Portugaise, mais elle a **un nom** français.
I thought she was Portugese, but she has a French **name**.

170- Une famille – *A family*

J'ai **une famille** étrange, mais je l'aime quand même.
I have a strange **family**, but I love it nonetheless.

171- Un effet – *An effect*

Paul sait comment se faire remarquer, il a vraiment **un effet** sur les gens.
Paul knows how to get noticed, he really has **an effect** on people.

172- Une affaire – *A matter*

Je vais te rappeler plus tard, j'ai **une affaire** importante à régler.
I will call you back later, I have an important **matter** to address.

173- Arriver – *To arrive*

Puisque nous sommes partis à sept heures, nous allons **arriver** vers le dîner.
Because we left at seven o'clock, we will **arrive** around dinner.

174- Servir – *To serve*

Dans mon cours de cuisine, j'apprendrai à **servir** les meilleurs plats.

In my cooking class, I will learn **to serve** the best dishes.

175- Un mois – *A month*

J'irai voir un concert à Toronto dans **un mois**.

I will go see a concert in Toronto in **a month**.

176- Jamais – *Never*

De quoi parles-tu? Je n'ai **jamais** entendu parler d'une telle chose.

What are you talking about? I have **never** heard of such a thing.

177- Car – *Because*

Je n'ai pas pu prendre ton appel, **car** j'étais dans la douche.

I could not take your call **because** I was in the shower.

178- Possible – *Possible*

Tout est **possible** lorsqu'on travaille assez fort.

Everything is **possible** when one works hard enough.

179- Tant – *So much/So many*

Mon père est extrêmement généreux; je l'aime **tant**.

My father is extremely generous; I love him **so much**.

180- Vers – *Towards*

Envoies la balle **vers** moi! Je sais que je peux marquer!

Kick the ball **towards** me! I know I can score!

181- Un besoin – *A need*

J'ai **un besoin** urgent de mettre de l'argent de côté pour mon voyage cet été.

I have an urgent **need** to put some money aside for my trip this summer.

182- Revenir – *To come back*

Il est parti ce matin et il va seulement **revenir** dans deux mois.
He left this morning and he will only **come back** in two months.

183- Sembler – *To seem*

Je te l'ai dit vingt fois, mais tu ne **sembles** pas comprendre.
I told you twenty times, but you don't **seem** to understand.

184- Un moyen – *A means*

L'autobus est **un moyen** de transport que je préfère éviter.
The bus is **a means** of transportation that I prefer to avoid.

185- Un groupe – *A group*

Un de mes collègues enseigne à **un groupe** de trente-deux élèves.
One of my colleagues teaches **a group** of thirty-two students.

186- Un problème – *A problem*

J'aimerais que tu m'aides à résoudre **un problème**.
I would like you to help me solve **a problem**.

187- Un rapport – *A report*

Je dois aller au bureau, j'ai **un rapport** à remettre à mon patron.
I need to go to the office, I have **a report** to hand over to my boss.

188- Dès que – *As soon as*

Je commence à m'inquiéter, appelle-moi **dès que** tu arrives à l'hôtel.
I'm starting to get worried, call me **as soon as** you get to the hotel.

189- Peut-être – *Maybe*

Peut-être que tu devrais arrêter de croire tout ce que Pierre te dit.
Maybe you should stop believing everything Pierre tells you.

190- Maintenant – *Now*

Elle part demain, alors c'est **maintenant** ou jamais!
She leaves tomorrow, so it's **now** or never!

191- Pourquoi – *Why*

Pourquoi crois-tu que les voisins déménagent?
Why do you think the neighbors are moving?

192- Meilleur|Meilleure – *Best*

Elle est la **meilleure** pianiste que j'aie entendue depuis longtemps.
She is the **best** pianist I have heard in a long time.

193- Une vue – *A view*

Nous aimerions réserver une chambre avec **une vue** sur la mer.
We would like to reserve a room with **a view** on the sea.

194- Trop – *Too much/Too many*

Tu t'en fais **trop** avec des choses sans importance.
You worry **too much** about unimportant things.

195- Laisser – *To let/To leave (something or someone)*

Yves m'a dit qu'il allait me **laisser**. Apparemment, je suis «
incapable de le **laisser** travailler en paix ».
Yves told me he was going **to leave** me. Apparently, I'm "unable
to let him work in peace".

196- Un ordre – *An order*

Range ta chambre, c'est **un ordre**!
Clean your room, that's **an order**!

197- Devant – *In front of*

Je n'ai rien pu voir, car il y avait trop de personnes **devant** moi.
I could not see anything, because there were too many people **in front of** me.

198- Recevoir – *To receive*

Je m'entraîne tous les jours pour **recevoir** cette médaille d'excellence.
I train everyday in order **to receive** this medal of excellence.

199- Répondre – *To answer*

Je ne peux pas **répondre** à toutes tes questions.
I can't **answer** all of your questions.

200- Long|Longue – *Long*

J'ai passé une **longue** journée au bureau, j'ai besoin de me détendre.
I had a **long** day at the office, I need to relax.

201- Un service – *A service/A favor*

Rendez-vous **service** et offrez un meilleur **service** à la clientèle!
Do yourself **a favor** and offer a better customer **service**!

202- Un|Une ministre – *A minister*

Nous avons réellement besoin d'un **ministre** de l'Éducation qualifié.
We really need a qualified **minister** of Education.

203- Vivre – *To live*

Je préfèrerais **vivre** à la campagne qu'au centre-ville.
I would rather **live** in the countryside than in the city center.

204- Chez – *At/To (someone's)*

On peut manger **chez** moi ou on peut aller **chez** Marie-Ève.
We can eat **at** my place or we can go **to** Marie-Ève**'s**.

205- Te – *Yourself*

Tu **te** coupes toujours avec ce couteau de cuisine, fais attention!
You always cut **yourself** with this kitchen knife, be careful!

206- Rappeler – *To call back/To remind of*

Je dois **rappeler** Jasmine pour lui **rappeler** de ne pas oublier ses clés.
I need **to call** Jasmine **back to remind** her not to forget her keys.

207- En face de – *In front of*

Elle était **en face de** moi, mais je n'ai pas été capable de lui dire la vérité.
She was **in front of** me, but I was not able to tell her the truth.

208- Accepter – *To accept*

Tu dois **accepter** mon invitation pour qu'on puisse jouer en ligne ensemble.
You need **to accept** my invitation so we can play online together.

209- Agir – *To act*

Si tu ne peux pas **agir** de façon appropriée, on rentre à la maison.
If you can't **act** appropriately, we are going back home.

210- Simple – *Simple*

J'aimerais devenir médecin, mais ce n'est pas si **simple**.
I'd like to become a doctor, but it's not that **simple**.

211- Présenter – *To present*

J'ai plusieurs théories scientifiques à vous **présenter**.
I have several scientific theories **to present** to you.

212- Votre – *Your (Formal)*

Puis-je avoir **votre** numéro de téléphone s'il-vous-plaît?
Can I please have **your** phone number?

213- Important|Importante – *Important*

Cette voiture est très **importante** pour moi, elle appartenait à mon père.
This car is very **important** to me, it belonged to my father.

214- Présent|Présente – *Present*

Amélie n'était pas **présente** en classe aujourd'hui, est-elle malade?
Amélie was not **present** in class today, is she sick?

215- Mieux – *Better*

Si tu veux gagner la médaille d'or, tu devras faire **mieux**.
If you want to win the gold medal, you will need to do **better**.

216- Plusieurs – *Several*

J'aime beaucoup ce restaurant, j'y suis allée **plusieurs** fois.
I like this restaurant a lot, I have been there **several** times.

217- Jouer – *To play*

Je n'ai pas le temps de **jouer** aux jeux vidéos avec toi en ce moment.
I don't have time **to play** video games with you right now.

218- Un mot – *A word*

J'apprends au moins un nouveau **mot** chaque jour.
I learn at least one new **word** each day.

219- Reconnaître – *To recognize*

Ma mère est très âgée, il lui est parfois difficile de me **reconnaître**.
My mother is very old, it's sometimes difficult for her **to recognize** me.

220- Poser – *To pose/To ask*

J'ai quelques questions à vous **poser**. Cela va-t-il **poser** problème?
I have some questions **to ask** you. Will this **pose** a problem?

221- Une situation – *A situation*

Je me suis retrouvée dans une très mauvaise **situation**.
I found myself in a very bad **situation**.

222- Offrir – *To offer*

Je n'ai pas beaucoup à t'**offrir**, mais je t'aime de tout mon cœur.
I don't have a lot **to offer** you, but I love you with all my heart.

223- Près – *Near/Close*

Attends-moi **près** de la sortie, nous partirons ensemble.
Wait for me **near** the exit, we'll leave together.

224- Une force – *A force*

Je détecte la présence d'**une force** surnaturelle dans cette pièce.
I detect the presence of a supernatural **force** in this room.

225- National|Nationale – *National*

Au Québec, la Fête **nationale** est le 24 juin.
In Quebec, the **National** Holiday is on June 24th.

226- Un projet – *A project*

Un de mes amis m'a parlé d'**un projet** intéressant.
One of my friends told me about an interesting **project**.

227- Ni... ni – *Nor*

Je n'aime **ni** le foot, **ni** le baseball.
I don't like soccer **nor** baseball.

228- Choisir – *To choose*

Tu dois **choisir** quelque chose sur le menu, le serveur arrive!
You need **to choose** something on the menu, the waiter is coming!

229- Toucher – *To touch*

Il est interdit de **toucher** les artéfacts au musée.
It is forbidden **to touch** the artefacts at the museum.

230- Le train – *The train*

Le train coûte beaucoup moins cher qu'un taxi.
The train costs a lot less than a taxi.

231- Aujourd'hui – *Today*

J'ai beaucoup de choses à faire **aujourd'hui**.
I have a lot of things to do **today**.

232- Comment – *How*

Ce livret explique **comment** assembler le bureau.
This booklet explains **how** to assemble the desk.

233- Puis – *Then*

Elle a lavé sa voiture, **puis** elle est sortie avec amis.
She washed her car, **then** she went out with friends.

234- Des gens – *People*

Il y avait **des gens** en colère devant le Parlement ce matin.
There were angry **people** in front of the Parliament this morning.

235- Propre – *Clean/Proper*

Je m'assure que mon appartement soit toujours **propre**.
I make sure that my apartment is always **clean**.

236- Grâce à – *Thanks to*

Je me sens tellement mieux **grâce** à toi.
I feel so much better **thanks to** you.

237- Une idée – *An idea*

Geneviève a une excellente **idée** pour notre projet d'équipe.
Geneviève has an excellent **idea** for our team project.

238- Surtout – *Especially*

J'adore les chiens, **surtout** les labradors.
I love dogs, **especially** Labrador Retrievers.

239- Une région – *A region*

Ma grand-mère habite dans **une région** où il n'y a pas de réseau téléphonique.
My grandmother lives in **a region** where there is no phone service.

240- Aimer – *To like/To love*

Il est difficile d'**aimer** quelqu'un en qui on ne peut pas avoir confiance.
It's hard **to love** someone you can't trust.

241- Un sens – *A sense*

Dans **un sens**, il est vrai que la philosophie est un sujet complexe.
In **a sense**, it's true that philosophy is a complex subject.

242- Selon – *According to*

Selon cet article, plusieurs animaux marins n'ont pas encore été découverts.

According to this article, many marine animals have not been discovered yet.

243- Une semaine – *A week*

Simon est nerveux, car son examen de conduite est dans **une semaine**.

Simon is nervous, because his driving exam is in **a week**.

244- Également – *Also*

Hugo est **également** un peintre amateur.

Hugo is **also** an amateur painter.

245- Celui-ci|Celle-ci – *This one*

J'ai déjà une voiture, mais je préfère **celle-ci**.

I already have a car, but I prefer **this one**.

246- Retrouver – *To find (something or oneself)*

J'ai perdu mon chat; pouvez-vous m'aider à le **retrouver**?

I lost my cat; can you help me **find** it?

247- Un nombre – *A number*

Nous sommes entourés d'**un nombre** élevé de spectateurs.

We are surrounded by a high **number** of spectators.

248- Perdre – *To lose*

J'aime jouer mais je n'aime pas **perdre**.

I like to play but I don't like **to lose**.

249- Le français – *French*

Le français a été créé il y a des centaines d'années.
French was created hundreds of years ago.

250- Une façon – *A way/A manner*

Connais-tu **une façon** efficace de régler ce problème?
Do you know an efficient **way** to solve this problem?

251- Quatre – *Four*

J'ai **quatre** frères et une sœur.
I have **four** brothers and one sister.

252- Un compte – *An account*

Je viens d'ouvrir **un compte** avec cette banque.
I have just opened **an account** with this bank.

253- Considérer – *To consider*

Tu ne peux pas vraiment le **considérer** comme un ami.
You can't really **consider** him as a friend.

254- Expliquer – *To explain*

C'est compliqué, je ne sais pas comment l'**expliquer**.
It's complicated, I don't know how **to explain** it.

255- Ouvrir – *To open*

Surveille le chien, je vais **ouvrir** la porte.
Watch the dog, I'm going to **open** the door.

256- Gagner – *To win*

Je vais **gagner** cette partie d'échecs, j'en suis certain.
I will **win** this game of chess, I'm certain of it.

257- Un exemple – *An example*

Je ne comprends pas, peux-tu me donner **un exemple**?
I don't understand, can you give me **an example**?

258 – Lorsque – *When*

J'étais au bureau **lorsque** j'ai entendu la nouvelle.
I was at the office **when** I heard the news.

259- Économique – *Economic/Economical*

L'autobus est un moyen de transport **économique**.
The bus is an **economical** means of transportation.

260- Une mesure – *A measure*

Le gouvernement sauve beaucoup d'argent avec cette **mesure**.
The government is saving a lot of money with this **measure**.

261- Une histoire – *A history/A story*

L'**histoire** est ma matière favorite après la littérature; j'adore lire et écrire des **histoires**.
History is my favorite subject after literature; I love to read and write **stories**.

262- Une ville – *A city*

J'habite dans **une ville** où il y a beaucoup de citoyens.
I live in **a city** where there is a lot of citizens.

263- Ensuite – *Next*

Que vas-tu faire **ensuite**?
What will you do **next**?

264- Une guerre – *A war*

Commencer **une guerre** n'est pas un bon moyen de régler les choses.

Starting **a war** is not a good way to settle things.

265- La loi – *The law*

Tu ne peux pas te stationner ici, c'est **la loi**.
You can't park here, it's **the law**.

266- Président|Présidente – *President*

Le **président** du comité a beaucoup à nous apprendre.
The **president** of the committee has a lot to teach us.

267- Le haut – *The top*

Écris ton nom dans **le haut** de la feuille.
Write your name at **the top** of the sheet.

268- Sûr|Sûre – *Sure*

Es-tu **sûre** qu'il soit parti par là?
Are you **sure** he went that way?

269- Refuser – *To refuse*

Mon patron m'a fait une offre que je ne peux pas **refuser**.
My boss made me an offer I can't **refuse**.

270- Plutôt – *Rather*

Je crois que ça s'est **plutôt** bien déroulé.
I believe it went **rather** well.

271- Un bureau – *A desk/An office*

Quand je suis au **bureau**, je passe des heures assis à mon **bureau**.
When I'm at **the office**, I spend hours sitting at my **desk**.

272- Exister – *To exist*

Bientôt, certaines langues cesseront d'**exister**.
Soon, some languages will cease **to exist**.

273- Quant à – *As for*

Julien aime le cinéma; **quant à** Martine, elle préfère la photographie.
Julien likes cinema; **as for** Martine, she prefers photography.

274- Mort|Morte – *Dead*

Sa femme l'a laissé, il a perdu son emploi et maintenant sa mère est **morte**.
His wife left him, he lost his job and now his mother is **dead**.

275- Mal – *Bad*

Je me sens **mal** pour Fannie, je devrais aller lui parler.
I feel **bad** for Fannie, I should go talk to her.

276- Mauvais|Mauvaise – *Wrong*

J'ai encore eu la **mauvaise** réponse à cette question.
I got the **wrong** answer to this question again.

277- Réussir – *To succeed*

Si tu pratiques tous les jours, tu vas **réussir**.
If you practice everyday, you'll **succeed**.

278- Un marché – *A market*

Le **marché** de l'assurance est très lucratif.
The insurance **market** is very lucrative.

279- Une condition – *A condition*

J'irai avec toi à **une condition** : je conduis la voiture.
I'll go with you under **one condition**: I'm driving the car.

280- Lire – *To read*

Assurez-vous de **lire** les instructions avant de commencer.
Make sure you **read** the instructions before you begin.

281- Changer – *To change*

Il est trop tard pour **changer** d'avis.
It's too late **to change** your mind.

282- Oui – *Yes*

Oui, c'est moi qui ai mangé la dernière part de gâteau.
Yes, I'm the one who ate the last piece of cake.

283- Un public – *A public/An audience*

Il a joué devant **un public** de deux cents personnes.
He played in front of **an audience** of two hundred people.

284- Humain|Humaine – *Human*

J'ai fait une erreur; je suis **humaine** après tout.
I made a mistake; I'm **human** after all.

285- International|Internationale – *International*

Je suis sur un vol **international** qui se dirige vers Sydney.
I am on an **international** flight directed to Sydney.

286- Cinq – *Five*

On se reverra dans **cinq** jours.
We'll see each other again in **five** days.

287- Un système – *A system*

Nous avons besoin d'un meilleur **système** de gestion.
We need a better management **system**.

288- Travailler – *To work*

Je n'ai pas le temps, je dois **travailler**.
I don't have the time, I need **to work**.

289- Souvent – *Often*

Je ne vois pas ma famille assez **souvent**.
I don't see my family **often** enough.

290- Vrai|Vraie – *True*

Il est **vrai** que j'aurais pu me coucher plus tôt.
It's **true** that I could have gone to sleep earlier.

291- Représenter – *To represent*

Qui cet avocat est-il censé **représenter**?
Who is this lawyer supposed **to represent**?

292- Une madame – *A madam/A lady*

Pardonnez-moi **madame**, vous avez oublié votre chapeau.
Pardon me **madam**, you forgot your hat.

293- Une société – *A society*

Mon oncle m'a dit qu'il y avait **une société** secrète en France.
My uncle told me that there was a secret **society** in France.

294- Un jeu – *A game*

Je gagne toujours à ce **jeu**.
I always win at this **game**.

295- Quoi – *What*

Quoi? Qu'est-ce que tu veux dire par là?
What? What do you mean by that?

296- Une entreprise – *A business*

D'ici deux ans, j'aurai ma propre **entreprise**.
Within two years, I'll have my own **business**.

297- Un coup – *A blow/A knock*

Il lui a donné **un coup** directement sur la mâchoire!
He delivered **a blow** directly to his jaw!

298- Difficile – *Difficult*

Ma sœur est très **difficile**, elle ne veut rien manger.
My sister is very **difficult**, she doesn't want to eat anything.

299- Un or – *Gold*

Ces boucles d'oreilles sont faites en **or** blanc.
These earrings are made of white **gold**.

300- Assurer – *To assure/To insure*

Je vous **assure** que vos **assurances** sont entre de bonnes mains avec nous.
I **assure** you that your **insurance** is in good hands with us.

301- Essayer – *To try*

J'ai envie d'**essayer** le jarret d'agneau.
I want **to try** the lamb shank.

302- Juste – *Just/Fair*

Je voulais **juste** être honnête avec toi… Ta réaction n'est pas **juste**!
I **just** wanted to be honest with you… Your reaction is not **fair**!

303- Étranger|Étrangère – *Foreigner*

Veuillez pardonner mon accent, je suis **étrangère**.
Please pardon my accent, I'm a **foreigner**.

304- Social|Sociale – *Social*

Je dois rencontrer une assistante **sociale** cette après-midi.
I have to meet a **social** worker this afternoon.

305- Un million – *A million*

J'ai déjà vu ce film **un million** de fois!
I have already seen this movie **a million** times!

306- Une manière – *A manner/A way*

Crier n'est pas **une manière** de régler les choses.
Yelling is not **a way** to solve things.

307- Sortir – *To go out/To leave*

Je dois absolument **sortir** de chez moi. Veux-tu **sortir** ce soir?
I absolutely need to **leave** my house. Do you want **to go out** tonight?

308- Empêcher – *To prevent*

Seul le protagoniste peut **empêcher** la fin du monde.
Only the protagonist can **prevent** the end of the world.

309- Un terme – *A term*

Ce **terme** a plus d'un sens.
This **term** has more than one meaning.

310- Longtemps – *A long time*

Je t'aime depuis **longtemps**, nous sommes faits l'un pour l'autre.
I have loved you for **a long time**, we're made for each other.

311- Reprendre – *To resume/To take back*

Nous allons **reprendre** à la page huit, mais d'abord, je vais
reprendre mon stylo rouge, Marie.
We'll **resume** on page eight, but first, I'll **take back** my red pen, Marie.

312- Le prix – *The price*

La solitude est **le prix** à payer pour réussir.
Solitude is **the price** to pay to succeed.

313- Un intérêt – *An interest*

J'ai toujous eu **un intérêt** pour la mode.
I have always had **an interest** in fashion.

314- Mener – *To lead*

Ce joueur va **mener** son équipe vers la victoire!
This player will **lead** his team to victory!

315- Une information – *Information*

Il me faut **une information** spécifique pour remplir ce formulaire.
I require specific **information** to fill in this form.

316- Courant|Courante – *Common*

Cette méthode est très **courante** en Amérique du Nord.
This method is very **common** in North America.

317- Appartenir – *To belong*

Cette paire de lunettes pourrait **appartenir** au coupable!
This pair of glasses could **belong** to the culprit!

318- La liberté – *The liberty/The freedom*

Tu as **la liberté** de t'en aller si c'est ce que tu veux.
You have **the freedom** to leave if that's what you want.

319- Assez – *Enough*

Je n'ai pas **assez** d'argent pour manger dans ce restaurant.
I don't have **enough** money to eat in this restaurant.

320- Un détail – *A detail*

Je ne comprends pas, j'ai besoin plus de **détails**.
I don't understand, I need more **details**.

321- Chacun – *Each*

Tu dois quinze dollars à **chacun** de nous pour le repas d'hier.
You owe **each** of us fifteen dollars for yesterday's meal.

322- Concerner – *To concern*

Mêle-toi de tes affaires, ça ne te **concerne** pas.
Mind your own business, this doesn't **concern** you.

323- Une maison – *A house*

Je viens d'acheter **une maison**; j'emménage avec ma femme dans un mois.
I just bought **a house**; I'm moving in with my wife in a month.

324- D'abord – *First/First of all*

Nous pouvons aller au cinéma, mais tu dois **d'abord** venir me chercher.
We can go to the movies, but you need to come get me **first**.

325- Risquer – *To risk*

Je préfère louer un casier et ne pas **risquer** de perdre mon portefeuille.
I prefer to rent a locker and not **risk** losing my wallet.

326- Un niveau – *A level*

Nous ne sommes pas au même **niveau**, toi et moi.
We are not on the same **level**, you and I.

327- Rencontrer – *To meet*

Rachel aimerait **rencontrer** le chanteur après le spectacle.
Rachel would like **to meet** the singer after the show.

328- Ton – *Your*

Est-ce que je pourrais emprunter **ton** tournevis?
Could I borrow **your** screwdriver?

329- Apprendre – *To learn*

Je veux **apprendre** à faire du vélo.
I want **to learn** how to ride a bike.

330- Créer – *To create*

Je sais qu'Élise est capable de **créer** des histoires magnifiques.
I know that Élise is able **to create** wonderful stories.

331- Un état – *A state*

David est dans un mauvais **état** d'esprit depuis que Sabrina l'a laissé.
David is in a bad **state** of mind since Sabrina left him.

332- Obtenir – *To obtain*

J'aurais aimé **obtenir** un résultat plus satisfaisant.
I would have liked **to obtain** a more satisfying result.

333- Une œuvre – *A work*

Cette exposition présente de nombreuses **œuvres** d'art splendides.
This exposition showcases many splendid **works** of art.

334- Chercher – *To search for*

Je **cherche** la rue Laurier; savez-vous où c'est?
I am **searching for** Laurier street; do you know where that is?

335- Entrer – *To enter*

Vous devez d'abord **entrer** dans la file d'attente.
You first need **to enter** the waiting line.

336- Proposer – *To offer*

J'ai une excellente suggestion à te **proposer**.
I have an excellent suggestion **to offer** you.

337- Clair|Claire – *Clear*

Le ciel est **clair** et les oiseaux chantent; quelle belle journée!
The sky is **clear** and the birds are singing; what a beautiful day!

338- Un programme – *A program*

Cet élève fait partie d'un **programme** sportif à son école.
This student is part of a sports **program** at his school.

339- Loin – *Far*

Mon grand-père habite très **loin** d'ici.
My grandfather lives very **far** from here.

340- Une ligne – *A line*

Il est important de savoir où tracer **la ligne**.
It's important to know where to draw **the line**.

341- Apporter – *To bring (something)*

N'oublis pas d'**apporter** ton chargeur cette fois-ci.
Don't forget **to bring** your charger this time.

342- Libre – *Free*

Son père est en prison, il sera **libre** dans six mois.
Her father is in prison, he will be **free** in six months.

343- Utiliser – *To use*

Ma grand-mère ne sait toujours pas comment **utiliser** un ordinateur.
My grandmother still doesn't know how **to use** a computer.

344- Atteindre – *To reach*

Je me suis fixé un objectif et j'arriverai à l'**atteindre**.
I set an objective for myself and I will be able **to reach** it.

345- Tenter – *To tempt/To try*

Ne **tente** pas de me **tenter** avec cette barre de chocolat!
Don't **try** to **tempt** me with this chocolate bar!

346- Une tête – *A head*

Si tu continues je vais te frapper derrière **la tête**.
If you keep going I'll hit you behind **the head**.

347- Enfin – *Finally*

J'ai terminé ma dissertation, **enfin**!
I finished my essay, **finally**!

348- Différent|Différente – *Different*

Tu as l'air **différente** depuis que tu es revenue de voyage.
You look **different** since you came back from your trip.

349- Une sorte – *A sort/A kind*

Quelle **sorte** d'homme recherches-tu?
What **kind** of man are you looking for?

350- Cependant – *However*

Tu peux arriver en avance; **cependant**, tu devras attendre dehors.
You can arrive ahead of time; **however**, you will need to wait outside.

351- Tard – *Late*

Je vais rentrer chez moi, il est déjà **tard**.
I will go back home, it's already **late**.

352- Importer – *To import/To matter*

Ça m'**importe** peu si le vin est local ou **importé**.
It doesn't **matter** to me if the wine is local or **imported**.

353- Une action – *An action*

Il devra répondre de ses **actions**.
He will need to answer for his **actions**.

354- Une relation – *A relationship*

Sylvain est dans **une relation** malsaine depuis trop longtemps.
Sylvain has been in an unhealthy **relationship** for too long.

355- Un sujet – *A subject*

J'ai essayé de lui en parler, mais elle a changé de **sujet**.
I tried to talk to her about it, but she changed the **subject**.

356- Un livre – *A book*

J'ai lu **un livre** très intéressant dans mon cours de français.
I read a very interesting **book** in my French class.

357- Ajouter – *To add*

Tu dois **ajouter** les œufs après la farine.
You have **to add** the eggs after the flour.

358- Ailleurs – *Elsewhere*

Même quand tu es avec moi, on dirait que tu es **ailleurs**.
Even when you're with me, it seems like you're **elsewhere**.

359- Vraiment – *Really/Very*

J'ai **vraiment** hâte de te voir demain.
I **really** can't wait to see you tomorrow.

360- Une recherche – *A research/A search*

Il est maintenant plus facile que jamais d'effectuer **une recherche** en ligne.
It is now easier than ever to conduct an online **research**.

361- Le reste – *The rest*

Je viendrai demain chercher **le reste** de mes choses.
I'll come by tomorrow to pick up **the rest** of my things.

362- Le début – *The beginning*

Je suis fatigué depuis **le debut** de la semaine.
I have been tired since **the beginning** of the week.

363- Une présence – *A presence*

Reste avec moi, ta **présence** est rassurante.
Stay with me, your **presence** is reassuring.

364- Un doute – *A doubt*

Je les ai vus s'embrasser; ils s'aiment, sans aucun **doute**.
I saw them kissing; they love each other, without a **doubt**.

365- Produire – *To produce*

Les vaches de mon oncle vont **produire** beaucoup de lait cette année.
My uncle's cows will **produce** a lot of milk this year.

366- Préparer – *To prepare*

Je vais **préparer** une petite surprise pour leur anniversaire de mariage.
I will **prepare** a little surprise for their wedding anniversary.

367- Une forme – *A shape*

Le tapis a **une forme** de diamant.
The carpet has a diamond **shape**.

368- Une décision – *A decision*

Ta **décision** affectera toute la famille.
Your **decision** will affect the entire family.

369- Nombreux|Nombreuse – *Numerous*

Je lui ai demandé de **nombreuses** fois de réparer la fenêtre.
I asked him **numerous** times to fix the window.

370- Dix – *Ten*

Va te coucher! Il est déjà **dix** heures!
Go to sleep! It's already **ten** o'clock!

371- Un produit – *A product*

Ce n'était que **le produit** de mon imagination.
It was only **the product** of my imagination.

372- Américain|Américaine – *American*

J'aime les voitures japonaises plus que les voitures **américaines**.
I like Japanese cars better than American cars.

373- Un rôle – *A role*

L'éducation joue **un rôle** important dans notre société.
Education plays an important **role** in our society.

374- Relever – *To face*

Pour vivre une vie excitante, tu devras **relever** des défis.
To live an exciting life, you will need **to face** challenges.

375- Un peuple – *A people*

Nous faisons tous partie du même **peuple**, alors pourquoi se battre?
We are all part of the same **people**, so why fight?

376- Second|Seconde – *Second*

C'est la **seconde** fois que j'oublis mes clés cette semaine.
It's the **second** time I forget my keys this week.

377- Une minute – *A minute*

Attends **une minute**… Est-ce que tu portes mes chaussures?
Wait **a minute**… Are you wearing my shoes?

378- Prochain|Prochaine – *Next*

Je ne suis pas libre aujourd'hui, on se verra la **prochaine** fois.
I'm not free today, we'll see each other **next** time.

379- Autant – *As much*

Je ne crois pas qu'il m'aime **autant** que je l'aime.
I don't think he loves me **as much** as I love him.

380- Écrire – *To write*

Vivianne m'a dit qu'elle voulait **écrire** une histoire de science-fiction.
Vivianne told me she wanted to **write** a science-fiction story.

381- Une position – *A position*

J'ai mal à l'épaule, car j'ai dormi dans **une position** inconfortable.
My soulder hurts, because I slept in an uncomfortable **position**.

382- Un développement – *A development*

Toute le monde doit contribuer au **développement** de la société.
Everyone has to contribute to the **development** of society.

383- Défendre – *To defend/To forbid*

Tu l'as frappé pour te **défendre**? Pourtant je t'ai toujours **défendu** de te battre.
You hit him **to defend** yourself? Yet I always **forbade** you from fighting.

384- Un|Une chef – *A leader*

Yannick est **le chef** de notre équipe pour le projet final.
Yannick is **the leader** of our team for the final project.

385- Particulier|Particulière – *Particular/Peculiar*

Cette fleur est très rare; sa couleur est **particulière**.
This flower is very rare; its color is **peculiar**.

386- Un effort – *An effort*

Ne t'en fais pas, tes **efforts** seront récompensés.
Don't worry, your **efforts** will be rewarded.

387- Parmi – *Among*

Laquelle préfères-tu **parmi** toutes ces options?
Which one do you prefer **among** all these options?

388- Un|Une membre – *A member*

Sophie est **une membre** importante de notre équipe de volleyball.
Sophie is an important **member** of our volleyball team.

389- Tirer – *To pull*

La porte est bloquée, tu dois **tirer** plus fort sur la poignée.
The door is blocked, you need **to pull** harder on the handle.

390- Une économie – *An economy*

Notre **économie** est de pire en pire avec les années.
Our **economy** is getting worse and worse as years go by.

391- Beau|Belle – *Beautiful*

Ta fille est très **belle**, quel âge a-t-elle?
Your daughter is very **beautiful**, how old is she?

392- Plein|Pleine – *Full*

Mon verre était **plein** il y a cinq minutes, que s'est-il passé?
My glass was **full** five minutes ago, what happened?

393- Juger – *To judge*

Tu n'as aucun droit de me **juger**.
You have no right **to judge** me.

394- Éviter – *To avoid*

Arrête de l'**éviter** et va lui parler avant qu'il ne soit trop tard.
Stop **avoiding** her and go talk to her before it's too late.

395- Ancien|Ancienne – *Ancient*

Des archéologues ont découvert une tombe très **ancienne**.
Archeologists have discovered a very **ancient** tomb.

396- Personnel|Personnelle – *Personal*

Je ne veux pas en parler, c'est trop **personnel**.
I don't want to talk about it, it's too **personal**.

397- Un titre – *A title*

J'ai terminé d'écrire mon poème, il ne me reste plus qu'à lui trouver **un titre**.
I finished writing my poem, now I only need to find **a title** for it.

398- Un soir – *An evening*

J'ai rendez-vous avec Céline ce **soir**.
I have a date with Céline this **evening**.

399- Un parti – *A party*

Sais-tu déjà pour quel **parti** politique tu vas voter?
Do you already know what political **party** you're going to vote for?

400- Unique – *Unique*

Chaque personne est **unique**.
Every person is **unique**.

401- Souhaiter – *To wish*

J'appelle pour vous **souhaiter** un joyeux anniversaire.
I'm calling **to wish** you a happy birthday.

402- Afin de – *In order to*

Tu devras courir **afin de** rattraper l'autobus.
You will need to run **in order to** catch the bus.

403- Un objet – *An object*

Cet **objet** est très important pour moi, je refuse de le vendre.
This **object** is very important to me, I refuse to sell it.

404- Malgré – *Despite/In spite of*

Malgré le fait que tu me manques, j'apprécie la solitude.
Despite the fact that I miss you, I appreciate the solitude.

405- Une période – *A period*

Jean peut retenir son souffle pendant une longue **période** de temps.
Jean can hold his breath for a long **period** of time.

406- Engager – *To hire*

Je crois que je vais **engager** l'autre candidat.
I think I'll **hire** the other candidate.

407- Une peine – *A sentence/A sorrow*

Ma mère a ressenti une très grande **peine** lorsqu'elle a appris que mon père servirait **une peine** de six ans pour un crime qu'il n'a pas commis.
My mother felt a great **sorrow** when she learned that my father would serve a six-year **sentence** for a crime he did not commit.

408- Parfois – *Sometimes*

Parfois, je rêve que je peux voler.
Sometimes, I dream that I can fly.

409- Lors – *During*

Je me suis endormie **lors** du film.
I fell asleep **during** the movie.

410- Sérieux|Sérieuse – *Serious*

Arrête de rire, je suis **sérieux**!
Stop laughing, I'm **serious**!

411- Aider – *To help*

Viens m'**aider** à changer la roue de mon vélo.
Come **help** me change the wheel on my bike.

412- Réaliser – *To realize/To achieve*

J'ai **réalisé** que si je travaillais assez fort, je pourrais **réaliser** mon rêve.
I **realized** that if I worked hard enough, I could **achieve** my dream.

413- Terminer – *To finish*

Tu pourras sortir jouer dès que tu auras **terminé** ton assiette.
You can go out to play as soon as you **finish** your plate.

414- Une base – *A base*

Il y a des milliers d'articles dans cette **base** de données.
There are thousands of items in this data**base**.

415- Espérer – *To hope*

Tout ce que nous pouvons faire, c'est **espérer**.
All we can do is **hope**.

416- Une main – *A hand*

Elle s'est brisé **la main** en skiant.
She broke her **hand** while skiing.

417- Une voix – *A voice*

Ce chanteur a la plus belle **voix** que j'aie entendue de ma vie.
This singer has the most beautiful **voice** I've heard in my entire life.

418- Arrêter – *To stop*

Si seulement ils pouvaient **arrêter** de crier tout le temps.
If only they could **stop** yelling all the time.

419- Le retour – *The return*

J'attends patiemment **le retour** de mon mari.
I patiently await my husband's **return**.

420- Prêt|Prête – *Ready*

Nous sommes déjà en retard, es-tu **prête** à partir?
We're already late, are you **ready** to leave?

421- Une occasion – *An opportunity*

Ce sera la parfaite **occasion** de leur montrer ton travail.
This will be the perfect **opportunity** to show them your work.

422- Gros|Grosse – *Big/Large*

Je veux un verre de lait et une **grosse** part de gâteau.
I want a glass of milk and a **large** piece of cake.

423- Regarder – *To watch*

Je vais **regarder** cette série télévisée dès que j'arrive à la maison.
I'll **watch** this TV series as soon as I arrive home.

424- La plupart – *Most/The majority*

La plupart des gens mettent du ketchup dans leurs hot dogs.
Most people put ketchup in their hot dogs.

425- Un|Une deuxième – *The second*

J'ai encore pleuré **la deuxième** fois que j'ai regardé cet épisode.
I cried again **the second** time I watched this episode.

426- Un résultat – *A result*

Tu as travaillé fort et ça paraît : **le résultat** est impressionnant.
You have worked hard and it shows: **the result** is impressive.

427- Député|Députée – *Deputy*

Je crois que ce **député** peut réellement faire une différence.
I think this **deputy** can really make a difference.

428- Une terre – *A land*

Karl veut acheter **une terre** en campagne et construire sa propre maison.
Karl wants to buy **a land** in the countryside and build his own house.

429- Valoir – *To be worth*

Dans quelques années, son autographe va **valoir** des centaines de dollars!
In a few years, his autograph will **be worth** hundreds of dollars!

430- Un dollar – *A dollar*

Il n'y a pas si longtemps, on pouvait prendre le bus pour moins d'**un dollar**.
Not so long ago, you could ride the bus for less than **a dollar**.

431- Un intérieur – *An interior*

L'intérieur de ce matelas est rempli de mousse mémoire.
The interior of this mattress is filled with memory foam.

432- Écouter – *To listen to*

J'aime **écouter** cette chanson avant de m'endormir.
I like **to listen to** this song before falling asleep.

433- Une confiance – *Confidence/Trust*

Il faut d'abord avoir **confiance** en soi pour pouvoir donner sa
confiance à quelqu'un d'autre.
You first need to have **confidence** in yourself in order to be able to
give your **trust** to someone else.

434- Un choix – *A choice*

Penses-y, car bientôt tu devras faire **un choix**.
Think about it, because soon you'll need to make **a choice**.

435- Prévoir – *To anticipate*

Il faut **prevoir** qu'elle ne reagit pas de cette facon.
You must anticipate that she will not react this way.

436- Une page – *A page*

J'ai presque terminé ce livre, il me reste **une page** à lire.
I almost finished this book, I have **one page** left to read.

437- Notamment – *Notably*

Cette actrice a **notamment** remporté un Oscar l'an dernier.
This actress **notably** won an Oscar last year.

438- Un type – *A type*

Quel **type** de bois préfères-tu : le cerisier ou l'acajou?
What **type** of wood do you prefer: cherrywood or mahogany?

439- Un but – *A goal*

Son **but** pour cette saison est de marquer au moins trente **buts**.
His **goal** for this season is to score at least thirty **goals**.

440- Une chance – *A chance*

Gagner à ce jeu n'est qu'une question de **chance**.
Winning at this game is only a matter of **chance**.

441- Grave - *Serious*

L'accident était moins **grave** qu'elle le pensait.
The accident was less **serious** than she thought.

442- Une prise – *A catch*

J'ai fait une très belle **prise** en pêchant aujourd'hui!
I made a really nice **catch** while fishing today!

443- Européen|Européenne – *European*

La mode **européenne** est parfois très étrange.
European fashion is sometimes very strange.

444- Une étude – *A study*

J'effectue **une étude** sur les aptitudes des chiens âgés.
I am conducting **a study** on the abilities of elder dogs.

445- Un matin – *A morning*

Je me suis réveillée ce **matin** et tu étais déjà parti.
I woke up this **morning** and you were already gone.

446- Remplacer – *To replace*

Cette pièce est défectueuse, tu devras la **remplacer**.
This part is defective, you'll need **to replace** it.

447- Avancer – *To move forward*

C'est votre tour, veuillez **avancer**.
It's your turn, please **move forward**.

448- Six – *Six*

Quand j'avais **six** ans, je voulais devenir archéologue.
When I was **six** years old, I wanted to become an archeologist.

449- Nécessaire – *Necessary*

Ce sac contient tout le matériel **nécessaire** pour assembler la chaise.
This bag contains all **necessary** material to assemble the chair.

450- Une activité – *An activity*

L'**activité** physique est une partie importante de ma routine.
Physical **activity** is an important part of my routine.

451- Une valeur – *A value*

Ce collier a beaucoup de **valeur** sentimentale.
This necklace has a lot of sentimental **value**.

452- Un principe – *A principle*

Je ne peux pas faire ça, c'est contre mes **principes**.
I can't do that, it's against my **principles**.

453- Entier|Entière – *Whole/Entire*

Ma vie **entière** est dédiée à ma carrière.
My **whole** life is dedicated to my career.

454- Une réponse – *An answer*

J'ai besoin d'**une réponse** avant mercredi matin.
I need **an answer** before Wednesday morning.

455- Une aide – *Help*

J'ai besoin de ton **aide** pour un nouveau projet artistique.
I need your **help** for a new artistic project.

456- Marquer – *To mark*

Donne-moi une minute, je vais le **marquer** dans mon agenda.
Give me a minute, I'll **mark** it in my agenda.

457- Élever – *To raise*

Je ne crois pas que tu sois prêt à **élever** des enfants.
I don't think you're ready **to raise** children.

458- Pourtant – *Yet*

Tu m'as dit que tu serais à l'heure, **pourtant** tu ne l'étais pas.
You told me you'd be on time, **yet** you weren't.

459- Une commission – *A commission*

Le gouvernement devrait investir plus de fonds dans cette **commission**.
The government should invest more funds in this **commission**.

460- Cesser – *To cease*

Certaines langues vont éventuellement **cesser** d'exister.
Some languages will eventually **cease** to exist.

461- Poursuivre – *To pursue*

Olivier a décidé de quitter son emploi pour **poursuivre** son rêve d'enfance.
Olivier decided to quit his job **to pursue** his childhood dream.

462- Maintenir – *To maintain*

J'aimerais **maintenir** une bonne relation de travail avec ce client.
I would like **to maintain** a good business relationship with this client.

463- Principal|Principale – *Principal/Main*

L'histoire est la raison **principale** pour laquelle je veux voyager.
History is the **main** reason why I want to travel.

464- Exprimer – *To express*

Je trouve que c'est difficile d'**exprimer** mes sentiments.
I find it hard **to express** my feelings.

465- Ami|Amie – *Friend*

Mon meilleur **ami** étudie à l'étranger.
My best **friend** studies abroad.

466- Bas|Basse – *Low*

Nous ne pouvons quitter cet endroit lorsque la marée est aussi **basse**.
We can't leave this place when the tide is so **low**.

467- Une époque – *A time/An era*

La technologie de l'information a marqué le début d'une nouvelle **époque**.
Information technology marked the beginning of a new **era**.

468- Une moitié – *A half*

Vas-tu manger l'autre **moitié** de ta pomme?
Are you going to eat the other **half** of your apple?

469- Un avenir – *A future*

Je vous souhaite un merveilleux **avenir** ensemble.
I wish you a wonderful **future** together.

470- Un argent – *Money/Silver*

Cette chaîne en **argent** doit coûter beaucoup d'**argent**.
This **silver** chain must cost a lot of **money**.

471- Imposer – *To impose*

Il est normal pour un employeur d'**imposer** des règles strictes.
It's normal for an employer **to impose** strict rules.

472- Un œil – *An eye*

Peux-tu garder un **œil** sur Sara pendant quelques minutes?
Can you keep an **eye** on Sara for a few minutes?

473- De l'eau – *Water*

L'eau était si claire qu'on pouvait voir le fond.
The water was so clear that we could see the bottom.

474- Sauf – *Except*

Est-ce que tu viens? Tout le monde est prêt **sauf** toi!
Are you coming? Everbody is ready **except** you!

475- Une école – *A school*

Ma tante veut choisir une bonne **école** pour ses enfants.
My aunt wants to choose a good **school** for her children.

476- Une sécurité – *Security*

Redonne-moi ce que tu as pris ou j'appelle **la sécurité**.
Give me back what you took or I'm calling **security**.

477- Le milieu – *The middle*

J'étais directement **au milieu** de la foule.
I was directly in **the middle** of the crowd.

478- Presque – *Almost*

Je suis **presque** arrivée; donne-moi dix minutes.
I'm **almost** there; give me ten minutes.

479- Une attention – *An attention*

J'ai quelque chose d'important à vous dire, puis-je avoir votre **attention**?
I have something important to tell you, may I have your **attention**?

480- Un cadre – *A frame*

Je placerai cette photo de nous dans **un cadre**.
I will place this photo of us inside **a frame**.

481- Une lettre – *A letter*

Je lui ai écrit **une lettre** qui révèle tous mes sentiments.
I wrote him **a letter** that reveals all my feelings.

482- Un mouvement – *A movement*

Cette ballerine est très talentueuse; ses **mouvements** sont si délicats.
This ballerina is very talented; her **movements** are so delicate.

483- Former – *To form*

Nous allons **former** une alliance pour lutter contre cette injustice.
We will **form** an alliance to fight against this injustice.

484- Conduire – *To drive*

Je ne peux pas **conduire** pendant deux semaines à cause de mon opération.

I can't **drive** for two weeks because of my operation.

485- Une règle – *A rule*

Si tu veux vivre sous mon toit, tu dois suivre mes **règles**.

If you want to live under my roof, you need to follow my **rules**.

486- Un poste – *A position*

Malheureusement, ce **poste** est déjà comblé.

Unfortunately, this **position** is already filled.

487- Une demande – *A request*

Ce n'est pas **une demande**, c'est un ordre!

This is not **a request**, it's an order!

488- Le futur – *The future*

Nous aimerions avoir des enfants dans **un futur** proche.

We would like to have children in the near **future**.

489- Un acte – *An act*

Il est en prison, parce qu'il a commis **un acte** criminel.

He is in prison, because he has committed a criminal **act**.

490- Disparaître – *To disappear*

Parfois, j'aimerais pouvoir faire **disparaître** toutes tes problèmes.

Sometimes, I would like to be able to make all your problems **disappear**.

491- Priver – *To deprive*

Cet hôpital refuse de **priver** les patients des meilleurs soins possible.

This hospital refuses **to deprive** the patients of the best possible care.

492- Constituer – *To constitute*

Tous tes efforts **constituent** déjà une amélioration.
All your efforts already **constitute** an improvement.

493- Le centre – *The center*

Le contour du tapis est bleu, mais **le centre** est beige.
The outline of the carpet is blue, but **the center** is beige.

494- Un milliard – *A billion*

Cette entreprise vaut **un milliard** de dollars.
This company is worth **a billion** dollars.

495- Lier – *To bind*

Lors de cette réaction chimique, les atomes vont se **lier** ensemble.
During this chemical reaction, the atoms will **bind** together.

496- Obliger – *To force*

J'aimerais que tu viennes avec moi mais je ne veux pas t'y **obliger**.
I would like for you to come with me, but I don't want **to force**
you to.

497- Un accord – *An agreement*

Vous n'avez pas respecté notre **accord**.
You have not respected our **agreement**.

498- Craindre – *To fear*

Viens avec moi, tu n'as rien à **craindre**!
Come with me, you have nothing to **fear**!

499- Un âge – *An age*

Elle a l'air si jeune, je n'arrive pas à deviner son **âge**.
She seems so young, I can't guess her **age**.

500- Déclarer – *To declare*

Avant que vous partiez, avez-vous quelque chose à **déclarer**?
Before you leave, do you have something to **declare**?

501- Oublier – *To forget*

Ce moment était magique, je ne vais jamais l'**oublier**.
This moment was magical, I'll never **forget** it.

502- Un propos – *A comment/A statement*

Ce **propos** n'avait rien à voir avec la question.
This **statement** had nothing to do with the question.

503- Un passé – *A past*

Elle a eu **un passé** très difficile, mais elle est heureuse aujourd'hui.
She had a very difficult **past**, but she's happy today.

504- Quitter – *To leave*

Je vais **quitter** le bureau autour de neuf heures ce soir.
I will **leave** the office around nine o'clock tonight.

505- Un bout – *An end*

Mon grand-père s'assoit toujours au **bout** de la table.
My grandfather always sits at the **end** of the table.

506- La population – *The population*

Cette décision est ce qu'il y a de mieux pour **la population**.
This decision is what's best for **the population**.

507- Le/La troisième – *The third*

C'est **la troisième** fois que Pierre a un accident de voiture.
It's **the third** time Pierre has a car accident.

508- Responsable – *Responsible*

Tu dois apprendre à être plus **responsable**.
You must learn to be more **responsible**.

509- Une route – *A road*

Quelle **route** vas-tu prendre pour aller en Gaspésie?
Which **road** will you take to go to Gaspésie?

510- Tôt – *Early*

Jessy est parti très **tôt** ce matin.
Jessy left very **early** this morning.

511- Lancer – *To throw*

Essaie de **lancer** le ballon plus loin.
Try **to throw** the ball further.

512- Toi – *You*

Est-ce que c'est **toi** qui as pris mes clés de voiture?
Is it **you** that took my car keys?

513- Une fonction – *A function*

Cette nouvelle télécommande a trop de **fonctions**.
This new remote control has too many **functions**.

514- Un emploi – *A job/A position*

Remplissez ce formulaire afin de postuler pour cet **emploi**.
Fill in this form in order to apply for this **position**.

515- Un objectif – *An objective*

Je devrais atteindre mon **objectif** d'ici trois semaines.
I should reach my **objective** within three weeks.

516- Une limite – *A limit*

Il y a **une limite** à ce que je peux tolérer.
There's **a limit** to what I can tolerate.

517- Le journal – *The newspaper*

Mon mari lit seulement **le journal** pour la section sports.
My husband only reads **the newspaper** for the sports section.

518- Annoncer – *To announce*

Marie et moi avons quelque chose d'important à **annoncer**.
Marie and I have something important **to announce**.

519- Lui-même – *Himself*

Aimes-tu notre table de cuisine? Jérôme l'a construite **lui-même**.
Do you like our kitchen table? Jérôme built it **himself**.

520- Un tour – *A turn*

Vas-y Louis, c'est à ton **tour** de jouer.
Go on Louis, it's your **turn** to play.

521- Voilà – *There (you go)*

Voilà! J'ai enfin terminé mon examen.
There! I finally finished my exam.

522- Une volonté – *A will*

Tu dois avoir **une volonté** de fer pour être aussi déterminé.
You must have an iron **will** to be so determined.

523- Envoyer – *To send*

Je t'ai **envoyé** un message hier soir, mais tu n'as pas répondu.
I **sent** you a message last night, but you didn't answer.

524 Paraître – *To appear/To seem*

Pardonnez-moi, je ne voulais pas **paraître** impoli.
Forgive me, I did not want **to appear** impolite.

525- Puisque – *Because*

Je vais me coucher tôt ce soir, **puisque** j'ai mal dormi hier.
I'll go to bed early tonight, **because** I didn't sleep well last night.

526- Établir – *To establish*

Nous devons **établir** des règles avant d'emménager ensemble.
We have **to establish** rules before moving in together.

527- Un changement – *A change*

Avant de publier cet article, je devrai faire quelques **changements**.
Before publishing this article, I'll need to make a few **changes**.

528- Garder – *To keep*

Je te l'ai prêté, je n'ai jamais dit que tu pouvais le **garder** indéfiniment!
I lent it to you, I never said you could **keep** it indefinitely!

529- Partager – *To share*

Je n'ai plus faim, veux-tu **partager**?
I'm not hungry anymore, do you want **to share**?

530- Interdire – *To forbid*

Je t'**interdis** d'utiliser ce ton avec moi, je mérite le respect.
I **forbid** you from using that tone with me, I deserve respect.

531- Finir – *To finish*

J'ai hâte de **finir** de travailler.
I can't wait **to finish** work.

532- Placer – *To place*

Si tu pouvais **placer** les assiettes sur la table, ça aiderait beaucoup.
If you could **place** the plates on the table, that would help a lot.

533- Une réalité – *A reality*

L'inflation est **une réalité** à laquelle nous devons tous faire face.
Inflation is **a reality** we must all face.

534- Payer – *To pay*

Va **payer** pendant que je vais chercher la voiture.
Go **pay** while I go get the car.

535- Un esprit – *A mind/A spirit*

Je croyais avoir entendu **un esprit**, mais ce n'était que **mon esprit** qui me jouait des tours.
I thought I heard **a spirit**, but it was only **my mind** playing tricks on me.

536- Un domaine – *A domain/A field*

Mes deux sœurs travaillent dans **le domaine** de la médecine.
My two sisters work in **the field** of medicine.

537- Diriger – *To direct*

Rémi **dirige** une grande entreprise.
Rémi **directs** a large business.

538- Sentir – *To feel/To smell*

Je ne me **sentais** pas bien après avoir **senti** cette odeur atroce.
I did not **feel** well after **smelling** this awful stench.

539- Une nature – *A nature*

J'aime beaucoup Samuel, car il a **une nature** très calme.
I like Samuel a lot, because he has a very calm **nature**.

540- Un régime – *A regime*

Ce **régime** parlementaire est rempli d'injustices.
This parliamentary **regime** is filled with inequities.

541- Charger – *To charge*

Malheureusement, je devrai vous **charger** du temps
supplémentaire.
Unfortunately, I will have **to charge** you overtime.

542- Noter – *To note*

Je vais le **noter** sur un morceau de papier pour ne pas oublier.
I'll **note** it on a piece of paper so I won't forget.

543- Un parent – *A parent*

Mon frère n'est pas prêt à devenir **un parent**.
My brother is not ready to become **a parent**.

544- Tomber – *To fall*

Il est normal de **tomber** en apprenant à faire du vélo.
It's normal **to fall** while learning how to ride a bike.

545- Un départ – *A departure*

Le départ est prévu pour dix-huit heures.
The departure is planned for six PM.

546- Mondial|Mondiale – *Global*

Cette entreprise a une portée **mondiale**.
This company has a **global** reach.

547- Court|Courte – *Short*

Frédéric a tiré la **courte** paille, c'est son tour!
Frédéric drew the **short** straw, it's his turn!

548- Disposer – *To dispose*

Cette alliance pourrait nous permettre de **disposer** de nombreuses ressources.

This alliance could allow us **to dispose** of numerous resources.

549- Une parole – *A word*

Mon frère ne tient jamais sa **parole**, je ne peux pas lui faire confiance.

My brother never keeps his **word**, I can't trust him.

550- Le fond – *The bottom*

Il y a un insecte au **fond** de la bouteille!

There is an insect at **the bottom** of the bottle!

551- Public|Publique – *Public*

Ce groupe organisera un concert **public** dans le parc.

This band will organize a **public** concert in the parc.

552- Entraîner – *To train*

Je fais de la gymnastique depuis des années, je m'**entraîne** tous les jours.

I have been doing gymnastics for years, I **train** everyday.

553- Faux|Fausse – *False*

Il n'a rien fait, ce sont de **fausses** accusations!

He didn't do anything, those are **false** accusations!

554- Un genre – *A type*

Je ne m'entends pas avec ce **genre** de personnes.

I don't get along with this **type** of person.

555- Une communauté – *A community*

Nous voulons que notre **communauté** se sente en sécurité.
We want our **community** to feel safe.

556- Intéresser – *To interest*

Merci, cette proposition m'**intéresse** beaucoup.
Thank you, this proposal **interests** me a lot.

557- C'est-à-dire – *In other words*

Béatrice est arachnophobe, **c'est-à-dire** qu'elle a peur des araignées.
Béatrice is arachnophobic; **in other words**, she is afraid of spiders.

558- Retenir – *To hold back/To remember*

Je n'arriverai jamais à **retenir** tout ça par cœur. Je ne sais pas ce qui me **retient** d'abandonner.
I can never **remember** all of this by heart. I don't know what's **holding me back** from giving up.

559- Une matière – *Matter/A subject*

La chimie est ma **matière** favorite. Ce semestre, nous étudierons comment **la matière** réagit au froid extrême.
Chemistry is my favorite **subject**. This semester, we will study how **matter** reacts to extreme cold.

560- Un sein – *A breast*

Ma tante s'est fait enlever **un sein** à cause de son cancer.
My aunt had **a breast** removed because of her cancer.

561- (De) la difficulté – *Difficulty*

J'ai de **la difficulté** à croire que cet homme ait soixante ans.
I have **difficulty** believing that this man is sixty years old.

562- Parvenir – *To achieve*

Gravir cette montagne est épuisant, je ne sais pas si je vais y **parvenir**.
Climbing this mountain is exhausting, I don't know if I'll **achieve** it.

563- Un corps – *A body*

Ma copine a **un corps** magnifique, je le lui rappelle tous les jours.
My girlfriend has a magnificent **body**, I remind her of it everyday.

564- Un appel – *A call*

Je n'ai pas pu prendre ton **appel**, j'étais occupée.
I could not take your **call**, I was busy.

565- Un cœur – *A heart*

Ce médecin effectuera une chirurgie à **coeur** ouvert.
This doctor will perform open-**heart** surgery.

566- Un sport – *A sport*

La gymnastique est **un sport** tres beau
Gymnastics is a very beautiful **sport**.

567- Un père – *A father*

Mon **père** est la personne la plus importante dans ma vie.
My **father** is the most important person in my life.

568- Une organisation – *An organization*

Notre **organisation** opère dans quarante pays différents.
Our **organization** operates in forty different countries.

569- Un secteur – *A sector*

Pour étudier dans ce **secteur**, il te faut d'excellentes notes.

To study in this **sector**, you need excellent grades.

570- Noir|Noire – *Black*

Tu ne peux pas porter des souliers blancs avec une chemise **noire**!
You can't wear white shoes with a **black** shirt!

571- Un événement – *An event*

C'est le plus gros **événement** de l'année, tout le monde sera là.
It's the biggest **event** of the year, everyone will be there.

572- Double – *Double*

Je voudrais un **double** espresso, s'il-vous-plaît.
I would like a **double** espresso, please.

573- Une unité – *A unit*

Cet ensemble de chaises comprend quatre **unités**.
This chair set contains four **units.**

574- Une nation – *A nation*

Notre **nation** devient de plus en plus accueillante.
Our **nation** is becoming more and more welcoming.

575- Un conseil – *Advice/A council*

J'ai quelques **conseils** pour le **conseil** étudiant.
I have some **advice** for the student **council.**

576- Soutenir – *Tu support*

Je serai toujours là pour te **soutenir** à travers les moments
difficiles.
I'll always be there **to support** you through hard times.

577- La paix – *Peace*

Je n'ai pas ressenti une telle **paix** d'esprit depuis longtemps.
I have not felt such **peace** of mind in a long time.

578- Convaincre – *To convince*

Comment puis-je vous **convaincre** de changer d'avis?
How can I **convince** you to change your mind?

579- Partout – *Everywhere*

Mon chien me suit **partout** dans la maison.
My dog follows me **everywhere** around the house.

580- Une direction – *A direction*

Dans quelle **direction** est notre hôtel?
In which **direction** is our hotel?

581- Manquer – *To miss*

Il est seulement parti depuis trois jours, mais il me **manque** terriblement.
He has only been gone for three days, but I **miss** him terribly.

582- Actuel|Actuelle – *Current*

Notre situation **actuelle** ne nous le permet pas.
Our **current** situation doesn't allow it.

583- Opposer – *To oppose*

La partie de ce soir **opposera** ces deux équipes.
Tonight's game will **oppose** these two teams.

584- Une nuit – *A night*

Je n'ai pas bien dormi du tout **la nuit** dernière.
I didn't sleep well at all last **night**.

585- Une journée – *A day*

Nous avons passé une très belle **journée** ensemble.
We spent a very nice **day** together.

586- D'ailleurs – *Besides*

D'ailleurs, je t'en avais déjà parlé hier.
Besides, I had already told you about it yesterday.

587- Traiter – *To treat*

Mon fils me **traite** avec beaucoup de respect.
My son **treats** me with a lot of respect.

588- Indiquer – *To indicate*

Ces traces de pas **indiquent** qu'il y a un ours dans les parages.
These footprints **indicate** that there's a bear in the area.

589- Signifier – *To mean*

Peux-tu m'expliquer ce que ce mot **signifie**?
Can you explain to me what this word **means**?

590- Une technique – *A technique*

Il est possible d'obtenir le même résultat avec différentes **techniques**.
It's possible to obtain the same result with different **techniques**.

591- Rapidement – *Rapidly*

La sortie est dans 50 mètres, tu dois changer de voie **rapidement**.
The exit is in 50 meters, you need to change lanes **rapidly**.

592- Autour – *Around*

Asseyons-nous **autour** du feu pour discuter.
Let's sit **around** the fire to chat.

593- Réduire – *To reduce*

Les étudiants veulent que le gouvernement **réduise** les frais de scolarité.

The students want the government **to reduce** tuition fees.

594- D'après – *According to*

D'après ma mère, il n'y a rien de plus important que la famille.

According to my mother, there's nothing more important than family.

595- Tuer – *To kill*

Ce monstre a **tué** trente innocents sans raison.

This monster **killed** thirty people for no reason.

596- Riche – *Rich*

Si j'étais **riche**, je voyagerais beaucoup plus souvent.

If I was **rich**, I would travel a lot more often.

597- Préférer – *To prefer*

J'adore les sushis, mais ma mère **préfère** le filet mignon.

I love sushi, but my mother **prefers** filet mignon.

598- Une rue – *A street*

Pouvez-vous me dire où est **la rue** Papineau?

Can you tell me where Papineau **street** is?

599- Bref|Brève – *Brief*

Notre rencontre a été **bref**, j'espère qu'on se reverra bientôt.

Our meeting was **brief**, I hope we'll see each other again soon.

600- La violence – *Violence*

La violence n'est jamais une option à considérer.

Violence is never an option to consider.

601- Un siècle – *A century*

Le français a beaucoup changé au cours du dernier **siècle**.
French has changed a lot during the last **century**.

602- Un article – *An article*

J'ai lu **un article** très intéressant dans le journal ce matin.
I read a very interesting **article** in the newspaper this morning.

603- Nommer – *To name*

Ma sœur va avoir un fils, elle veut le **nommer** Pierrot.
My sister is going to have a son, she wants **to name** him Pierrot.

604- Une qualité – *A quality*

La générosité est la plus belle **qualité** chez un homme.
Generosity is the most beautiful **quality** in a man.

605- Gauche – *Left*

Vous devrez tourner à **gauche** au troisième stop.
You will need to turn **left** at the third stop.

606- Une solution – *A solution*

L'alcool n'est pas **une solution** pour tes problèmes.
Alcohol is not **a solution** to your problems.

607- Une voie – *A lane*

Ce conducteur est dangereux, il est incapable de rester dans sa **voie**!
This driver is dangerous, he's incapable of staying in his **lane**!

608- Durer – *To last*

Ce canapé est fait pour **durer** avec ses matériaux de haute qualité.

This couch is built **to last** with its high-quality materials.

609- Canadien|Canadienne – *Canadian*

Ma mère est **Canadienne**, mais mon père est Allemand.
My mother is **Canadian**, but my father is German.
610- Une erreur – *A mistake*
Tu fais toujours la même **erreur**.
You always make the same **mistake**.

611- Livrer – *To deliver*

Je peux vous le **livrer** avant cinq heures ce soir.
I can **deliver** it to you before five o'clock this evening.

612- Capable – *Capable*

C'est impossible, ma fille n'est pas **capable** de faire une chose pareille.
It's impossible, my daughter isn't **capable** of doing such a thing.

613- Simplement – *Simply*

Tout **simplement,** je ne l'aime pas.
Put **simply,** I don't like him.

614- Se souvenir – *To remember*

Je **me souviens** du temps où nous jouions dehors près du lac.
I **remember** the time when we used to play outside by the lake.

615- Une conséquence – *A consequence*

Tu dois assumer les **conséquences** de tes actes.
You must face the **consequences** of your actions.

616- Large – *Wide*

Cette bibliothèque est trop **large** pour ma chambre.

This bookshelf is too **large** for my room.

617- Auprès – *Beside*

Viens t'assoir **auprès** de moi, je te lirai une histoire.
Come sit **beside** me, I'll read you a story.

618- Un succès – *Success*

Elle a eu beaucoup de **succès** à la télévision.
She's had a lot of **success** on television.

619- Un élément – *An element*

Cette catégorie comprend plusieurs **éléments** similaires.
This category contains many similar **elements**.

620- Local|Locale – *Local*

Je préfère acheter un produit **local** qu'un produit importé.
I prefer to buy a **local** product than an imported product.

621- Le contraire – *The opposite*

Charles dit une chose, mais sa copine dit **le contraire**.
Charles says one thing, but his girlfriend says **the opposite**.

622- Inviter – *To invite*

Nous aimerions vous **inviter** à notre mariage en septembre.
We would like **to invite** you to our wedding in September.

623- Un extérieur – *An exterior*

L'extérieur de cette couverture est fait en velours.
The exterior of this blanket is made of velvet.

624- Un pied – *A foot*

Tout le monde a **un pied** plus long que l'autre.

Everyone has **one foot** longer than the other.

625- Une mission – *A mission*

Ma **mission** est secrète, je ne peux rien te dire.
My **mission** is secret, I can't tell you anything.

626- Un été – *A summer*

Nous avons passé un très bel **été** en Italie.
We spent a wonderful **summer** in Italy.

627- Une fille – *A girl/A daughter*

Ma **fille** ne s'entend pas bien avec les autres **filles** de sa classe.
My **daughter** doesn't get along well with the other **girls** in her
class.

628- Répéter – *To repeat*

Ne m'oblige pas à le **répéter** une troisième fois.
Don't force me **to repeat** it a third time.

629- Un texte – *A text*

Richard a écrit **un texte** très touchant sur la Deuxième Guerre
mondiale.
Richard wrote a very touching **text** on World War II.

630- Un débat – *A debate*

Nous faisons souvent des **débats** en cours de français.
We often do **debates** in French class.

631- Une chambre – *A room*

Je vais étudier dans ma **chambre**, ne me dérangez pas!
I'm going to study in my **room**, don't bother me!

632- Une création – *A creation*

Elle m'a fait entendre sa dernière **création**.
She made me listen to her last **creation**.

633- Prouver – *To prove*

L'avocat n'a pas pu **prouver** son innocence.
The lawyer could not **prove** her innocence.

634- Acheter – *To buy*

Je ne sais pas quoi **acheter** pour son anniversaire.
I don't know what **to buy** for her birthday.

635- Profiter – *To take advantage*

Tu ne peux pas **profiter** de moi comme ça.
You can't **take advantage** of me like that.

636- Une production – *A production*

Ce film est **une production** indépendante.
This movie is an independent **production**.

637- Ignorer – *To ignore*

Sophie est dans tous mes cours, je ne peux pas l'**ignorer**.
Sophie is in all my classes, I can't **ignore** her.

638- Directeur|Directrice – *Director*

La directrice de ce film est Polonaise.
The director of this movie is Polish.

639- La santé – *Health*

Repose-toi, tu seras en bonne **santé** d'ici quelques jours.
Rest, you'll be in good **health** within a few days.

640- La justice – *Justice*

Paul est un représentant pour le ministère de la **justice**.
Paul is a representative for the Ministry of **Justice**.

641- Précis|Précise – *Precise*

Je ne comprends pas ton exemple; peux-tu être plus **précis**?
I don't understand your example; can you be more **precise**?

642- Fixer – *To set*

Nous avons **fixé** la date pour le 9 octobre.
We have **set** the date for October 9th.

643- Une mère – *A mother*

Jaqueline est **la mère** d'André.
Jaqueline is André's **mother**.

644- Une croissance – *A growth*

Notre entreprise est au milieu d'une **croissance** économique.
Our business is in the middle of an economical **growth**.

645- Un risque – *A risk*

Il y a **un risque** élevé qu'elle perde sa vue après l'opération.
There is a high **risk** that she'll lose her sight after the surgery.

646- Souffrir – *To suffer*

Aidez-le, il **souffre** depuis trop longtemps.
Help him, he has **suffered** for too long.

647- Estimer – *To estimate*

Pouvez-vous **estimer** le prix des rénovations?
Can you **estimate** the cost of the renovations?

648- Un endroit – *A place/A spot*

Il y a **un endroit** magnifique près de la rivière.
There is a magnificent **spot** near the river.

649- Un comité – *A committee*

Je partage l'opinion du **comité**.
I share the opinion of the **committee**.

650- Impossible – *Impossible*

Il est **impossible** d'être dans deux endroits au même moment.
It's **impossible** to be in two places at the same time.

651- Une arme – *A weapon*

Ils n'ont jamais retrouvé **l'arme** du crime.
They never found the murder **weapon**.

652- Véritable – *Real*

Ce collier est fait en or **véritable**.
This necklace is made of **real** gold.

653- Amener – *To bring*

Tu devais m'**amener** Stéphanie avant huit heures.
You were supposed **to bring** me Stéphanie before eight o'clock.

654- Viser – *To aim*

Mes bras sont trop courts, c'est difficile de **viser**.
My arms are too short, it's difficult **to aim**.

655- Retirer – *To remove*

Cette tablette est facile à **retirer** du mur.
This shelf is easy **to remove** from the wall.

656- Une preuve – *A proof*

Vous n'avez aucune **preuve** que j'étais sur la scène du crime.
You have no **proof** that I was on the crime scene.

657- Une image – *An image*

J'aimerais utiliser cette **image** comme fond d'écran.
I would like to use this **image** as my wallpaper.

658- Une date – *A date*

Le vingt-cinq mai est **la date** de notre anniversaire.
May twenty-fifth is **the date** of our anniversary.

659- À travers – *Through*

Nous devrons passer **à travers** le désert.
We will need to go **through** the desert.

660- Un contrôle – *A control*

Olivier n'a pas un bon **contrôle** de sa colère.
Olivier does not have a good **control** of his anger.

661- Total|Totale – *Total*

Il ressent un désespoir **total** depuis que Kim l'a laissé.
He feels **total** despair since Kim left him.

662- Conserver – *To keep*

Je vais **conserver** ce document pour te le faire signer plus tard.
I will **keep** this document to have you sign it later.

663- Réel|Réelle – *Real*

Cette situation est **réelle**, nous devons agir sans délais.
This situation is **real**, we must act without delay.

664- La campagne – *The countryside*

Nous passerons le weekend à **la campagne**.
We'll spend the weekend in **the countryside**.

665- Naître – *To be born*

Le fils de mon frère est censé d'etre **naître** demain.
My brother's son is supposed **to be born** tomorrow.

666- Énorme – *Enormous*

Il y a une **énorme** différence entre ces deux choses.
There is an **enormous** difference between these two things.

667- Tourner – *To turn*

Tu dois **tourner** la page.
You need **to turn** the page.

668- Participer – *To participate*

Je crois que je suis prête à **participer** à cette course.
I think I'm ready **to participate** in this race.

669- Vieux|Vieille – *Old*

Cette maison est très **vieille**, elle a été construite il y a cent ans.
This house is very **old**, it was built one hundred years ago.

670- Accorder – *To grant*

Je t'**accorde** la permission de sortir.
I **grant** you the permission to go out.

671- Respecter – *To respect*

Il est essentiel de **respecter** tes parents.
It's essential **to respect** your parents.

672- Un passage – *A passage*

Il y a **un passage** secret derrière la bibliothèque.
There is a secret **passage** behind the bookcase.

673- Essentiel|Essentielle – *Essential*

Avoir de bonnes notes est **essentiel** pour être accepté dans ce programme.
Having good grades is **essential** to be accepted in this program.

674- Adopter – *To adopt*

Je dois convaincre ma femme d'**adopter** ce chien.
I need to convince my wife **to adopt** this dog.

675- Rapide – *Quick*

J'ai besoin d'une solution **rapide** à mon problème.
I need a **quick** solution to my problem.

676- Environ – *About*

Il y a **environ** deux litres d'eau dans cette bouteille.
There is **about** two liters of water in this bottle.

677- Une expérience – *An experience*

Ce voyage était une merveilleuse **expérience**.
This trip was a wonderful **experience**.

678- Admettre – *To admit*

Il l'aime, mais il ne peut pas l'**admettre**.
He loves her, but he can't **admit** it.

679- Découvrir – *To discover*

Il y a tellement de choses à **découvrir** en Europe.
There are so many things **to discover** in Europe.

680- Subir – *To be subjected to*

Aimée a **subi** beaucoup d'événements difficiles l'an dernier.
Aimée has **been subjected to** a lot of difficult events last year.

681- Assister – *To attend*

Malheureusement, je ne pourrai pas **assister** au spectacle de ce soir.
Unfortunately, I won't be able **to attend** tonight's show.

682- Sénateur|Sénatrice – *Senator*

Cette décision a été prise par **le sénateur**.
This decision was taken by **the senator**.

683- Dépasser – *To go beyond*

La fête était très amusante, elle a **dépassé** mes attentes.
The party was very fun, it **went beyond** my expectations.

684- Affirmer – *To affirm*

Personne ne va nous croire, nous sommes les seuls à l'**affirmer**.
No one will believe us, we are the only ones who **affirm** it.

685- Couvrir – *To cover*

La musique est si forte que je dois **couvrir** mes oreilles!
The music is so loud I have **to cover** my ears!

686- Financer – *To finance*

J'ai un nouveau projet, mais j'ai besoin de ton aide pour le **financer**.
I have a new project, but I need your help **to finance** it.

687- Un processus – *A process*

L'adoption est devenue **un processus** très long.
Adoption has become a very long **process**.

688- Militaire – *Military*

Mon cousin fait partie des forces **militaires**.
My cousin is part of the **military** forces.

689- Frais|Fraîche – *Fresh*

Ces tomates ne sont pas **fraîches**.
These tomatoes aren't **fresh**.

690- Soumettre – *To submit*

Tu ne dois jamais **soumettre** d'informations personnelles par courriel.
You must never **submit** personal information by email.

691- Une industrie – *An industry*

La mode est **une industrie** qui change constamment.
Fashion is **an industry** that changes constantly.

692- Apparaître – *To appear*

Ce cycliste est **apparu** de nulle part!
This cyclist **appeared** out of nowhere!

693- Une responsabilité – *A responsibility*

Surveille ta petite sœur, elle est ta **responsabilité**.
Watch over your little sister, she's your **responsibility**.

694- Réserver – *To reserve*

Pour manger à ce restaurant, nous devons d'abord **réserver**.
To eat at this restaurant, we must **reserve** first.

695- Une porte – *A door*

J'ai entendu frapper à **la porte**.
I heard a knock on **the door**.

696- Une victime – *A victim*

Heureusement, **la victime** a survécu.
Fortunately, **the victim** survived.

697- Un territoire – *A territory*

La Gaule a longtemps été **un territoire** contesté.
Gaul was a contested **territory** for a long time.

698- Pauvre – *Poor*

Plusieurs parties de l'Afrique sont encore très **pauvres**.
Many parts of Africa are still very **poor**.

699- Un taux – *A rate*

Son **taux** horaire a récemment augmenté.
Her hourly **rate** recently increased.

700- Posséder – *To possess/To own*

Je **possède** un immeuble au centre-ville.
I **own** a building downtown.

701- Le matériel – *The equipment*

Ce sac contient tout **le matériel** nécessaire.
This bag contains all necessary **equipment**.

702- Cent – *Hundred*

J'ai cinq **cents** dollars dans mon portefeuille.
I have five **hundred** dollars in my wallet.

703- Constater – *To notice*

J'ai **constaté** que tu avais mis une chemise différente cette fois.
I **noticed** that you put on a different shirt this time.

704- Prononcer – *To pronounce*

Ton nom est difficile à **prononcer**.
Your name is hard **to pronounce**.

705- Organiser – *To organize*

Je dois absolument **organiser** mon classeur.
I absolutely need **to organize** my filing cabinet.

706- Blanc|Blanche – *White*

Ma fleur préférée est le lys **blanc**.
My favorite flower is the **white** lily.

707- Une origine – *An origin*

Quelles sont tes **origines**?
What are your **origins**?

708- Vendre – *To sell*

Je ne peux pas **vendre** cette bague, j'y suis trop attachée.
I can't **sell** this ring, I'm too attached to it.

709- Vite – *Fast/Quickly*

Nous devons **vite** partir de cet endroit.
We need to leave this place **fast**.

710- Un signe – *A sign*

Notre rencontre était **un signe** du destin.
Our meeting was **a sign** from heaven.

711- Dangereux|Dangereuse – *Dangerous*

Ce sport est très **dangereux** : Raphaël s'est brisé la cheville.
This sport is very **dangerous**: Raphaël broke his ankle.

712- Déplacer – *To move*

Pourriez-vous vous **déplacer** un peu vert la droite?
Could you **move** slightly to the right?

713- Une importance – *An importance*

Tu ne réalises pas l'**importance** de ce rendez-vous.
You don't realize the **importance** of this date.

714- Suffire – *To suffice*

J'ai seulement trois dollars, est-ce que ça va **suffire**?
I only have three dollars, will it **suffice**?

715- Un espoir – *A hope*

J'ai de l'**espoir** pour l'avenir.
I have **hope** for the future.

716- Davantage – *More*

Tu devrais rire **davantage**, c'est bon pour ta santé.
You should laugh **more**, it's good for your health.

717- Une langue – *A language*

J'ai toujours rêvé d'apprendre une nouvelle **langue**.
I always dreamed of learning a new **language**.

718- Une énergie – *An energy*

Je n'ai plus d'**énergie** après tout cet exercice.
I have no more **energy** after all this exercise.

719- Un réseau – *A network*

Avant de partager vos informations, assurez-vous d'être connecté au **réseau**.
Before sharing your information, make sure you're connected to

the **network**.

720- Mourir – *To die*

Nous allons tous **mourir** ici!
We're all going **to die** here!

721- Faible – *Weak*

Je suis trop **faible** pour me lever, peux-tu m'aider?
I'm too **weak** to get up, can you help me?

722- Employer – *To use*

Je refuse d'**employer** la force pour régler mes problèmes.
I refuse **to use** force to solve my problems.

723- Saisir – *To seize*

Tu dois absolument **saisir** cette opportunité.
You absolutely must **seize** this opportunity.

724- Spécial|Spéciale – *Special*

Elle est une personne très **spéciale** pour moi.
She's a very **special** person to me.

725- Accompagner – *To accompany*

Pourrais-tu m'**accompagner** aux toilettes?
Could you **accompany** me to the bathroom?

726- Actuellement – *Currently*

Je suis chez moi **actuellement**.
I'm **currently** at home.

727- Une union – *A union*

Notre mariage est **une union** symbolique.

Our wedding is a symbolic **union**.

728- Supposer – *To suppose*

Je **suppose** qu'il ne viendras pas ce soir.
I **suppose** he won't be coming tonight.

729- Une possibilité – *A possibility*

Tu dois considérer toutes les **possibilités**.
You need to consider all the **possibilities**.

730- Ceci – *This*

Je ne comprends pas **ceci**, pourriez-vous me donner un autre exemple?
I don't understand **this**, could you give me another example?

731- Exiger – *To demand*

J'**exige** que tu sortes les poubelles immédiatement.
I **demand** that you take out the trash immediately.

732- Intervenir – *To intervene*

Les gens avaient trop peur d'**intervenir**.
People were too afraid **to intervene**.

733- Un fils – *A son*

Mon **fils** est musicien, je suis si fière de lui.
My **son** is a musician, I'm so proud of him.

734- D'accord – *Alright*

D'accord, je vais m'occuper de ton chien ce weekend.
Alright, I'll take care of your dog this weekend.

735- Fournir – *To provide*

Je peux te **fournir** des provisions si tu en as besoin.
I can **provide** you with supplies if you need them.

736- Une différence – *A difference*

Crois-tu vraiment que tes actions vont faire **une différence**?
Do you really believe that your actions will make **a difference**?

737- Protéger – *To protect*

Je l'ai fait pour te **protéger**.
I did it **to protect** you.

738- Abandonner – *To give up*

Tu y es presque, tu ne peux pas **abandonner** maintenant!
You're almost there, you can't **give up** now!

739- Discuter – *To discuss*

Nous devons **discuter** de ce qui s'est passé hier soir.
We need **to discuss** what happened last night.

740- Battre – *To beat*

Mon frère me **bat** tout le temps à ce jeu, ce n'est pas juste!
My brother always **beats** me at this game, it's not fair!

741- Pire – *Worse*

Arrêtez de crier ou la situation sera **pire** qu'elle soit déjà.
Stop yelling or the situation will be **worse** than it already is.

742- Adresser – *To address*

J'aimerais lui **adresser** quelques questions.
I would like **to address** him a few questions.

743- Préciser – *To specify*

J'aimerais **préciser** que je travaille ici depuis huit ans.
I woud like **to specify** that I have been working here for eight years.

744- Une intervention – *An intervention*

L'**intervention** de la police était trop tard.
The police's **intervention** was too late.

745- Un avis – *An opinion*

J'ai le droit à mon **avis** et tu as le droit au tien.
I'm entitled to my **opinion** and you're entitled to yours.

746- Demeurer – *To remain/To live*

Cette maison **demeure** le plus bel endroit où j'ai jamais **demeuré**.
This house **remains** the most beautiful place I've ever **lived** in.

747- Un chiffre – *A number*

Tu écris tellement mal, je n'arrive pas à lire ce **chiffre**.
You write so badly, I can't read this **number**.

748- Consacrer – *To devote*

Michelle a décidé de se **consacrer** à l'aide humanitaire.
Michelle decided **to devote** herself to humanitarian aid.

749- Attirer – *To attract*

Ton parfum **attire** les moustiques!
Your perfurme **attracts** mosquitoes!

750- Divers|Diverse – *Diverse/Various*

Je ne l'ai pas invité pour **diverses** raisons.
I did not invite him for **various** reasons.

751- Appliquer – *To apply*

Tu dois **appliquer** une couche de peinture supplémentaire.
You need **to apply** an additional paint coat.

752- Frapper – *To hit*

Je ne comprends pas pourquoi elle m'a **frappé**, je n'ai rien fait!
I don't understand why she **hit** me, I didn't do anything!

753- Une peur – *A fear*

J'ai une terrible **peur** des hauteurs.
I have a terrible **fear** of heights.

754- Un parlement – *A parliament*

Allons nous promener devant **le Parlement**.
Let's go take a walk in front of **the Parliament**.

755- Remplir – *To fill*

Je vais **remplir** ma bouteille avant de partir.
I'm going **to fill** my bottle before I leave.

756- Forcer – *To force*

Si elle ne veut pas y aller, tu ne peux pas la **forcer**.
If she doesn't want to go, you can't **force** her.

757- Une lutte – *A struggle*

La dépression est **une lutte** constante pour Martine.
Depression is a constant **struggle** for Martine.

758- Naturel|Naturelle – *Natural*

Je suis jalouse de sa beauté **naturelle**.
I'm jealous of her **natural** beauty.

759- Un air – *An air*

Louis a dit qu'elle était vraiment belle; il y a de l'amour dans **l'air**!
Louis said she was very beautiful; love is in **the air**!

760- Auteur|Auteure – *Author*

Xavier rêve de devenir un grand **auteur**.
Xavier dreams of becoming a great **author**.

761- Fermer – *To close*

Il fait froid, peux-tu **fermer** la fenêtre?
It's cold, can you **close** the window?

762- Heureux|Heureuse – *Happy*

Je suis si **heureux** de t'avoir rencontrée.
I'm so **happy** to have met you.

763- Une crise – *A crisis*

Lors d'**une crise**, il est important de ne pas paniquer.
During **a crisis**, it's important not to panick.

764- Un numéro – *A number*

Donne-moi ton **numéro**, je t'appellerai plus tard.
Give me your **number**, I'll call you later.

765- Résoudre – *To solve*

Tu ne vas jamais **résoudre** tes problèmes avec cette attitude.
You will never **solve** your problems with that attitude.

766- Publier – *To publish*

Personne ne veut **publier** son article.
Nobody wants **to publish** her article.

767- Une opération – *An operation*

Tu devras te reposer après **l'opération**.
You will need to rest after **the operation**.

768- Toutefois – *However*

J'accepte de venir avec toi; **toutefois**, je devrai partir avant neuf heures.
I agree to go with you; **however**, I'll need to leave before nine o'clock.

769- Pousser – *To push*

Pas besoin de **pousser**, il y en aura pour tout le monde.
No need **to push**, there will be enough for everybody.

770- Quelqu'un – *Someone/Somebody*

Je n'avais jamais rencontré **quelqu'un** comme toi.
I had never met **someone** like you.

771- Un discours – *A speech*

Je dois préparer **un discours** pour le mariage de mon frère.
I must prepare **a speech** for my brother's wedding.

772- Une banque – *A bank*

Je n'ai plus d'argent liquide, je dois faire un arrêt à **la banque**.
I don't have any more cash, I need to make a stop at **the bank**.

773- Un instant – *An instant/A moment*

J'arrive dans **un instant**, attends-moi dehors.
I'll be there in **a moment**, wait for me outside.

774- Se reposer – *To rest*

Il est rentré tard hier soir, laisse-le **se reposer**.

He came home late last night, let him **rest**.

775- Une opinion – *An opinion*

Personne ne t'a demandé ton **opinion**.
Nobody asked for your **opinion**.

776- Une classe – *A class*

Je ne tolére pas ce comportement dans ma **classe**.
I do not tolerate this behavior in my **class**.

777- Particulièrement – *Particularly*

Ton sourire est **particulièrement** radieux aujourd'hui.
Your smile is **particularly** radiant today.

778- Commun|Commune – *Common*

Ce genre de comportement est très **commun** chez les chats.
This kind of behavior is very **common** among cats.

779- Une compagnie – *A company*

Ta **compagnie** est grandement appréciée pendant ce moment difficile.
Your **company** is greatly appreciated during this hard time.

780- Une intention – *An intention*

Ce n'était pas mon **intention** de te blesser.
It was not my **intention** to hurt you.

781- Une autorité – *An authority*

Dans cette classe, c'est moi la figure d'**autorité**.
In this class, I am the **authority** figure.

782- Anglais|Anglaise – *English*

La copine de mon oncle est **Anglaise**.
My uncle's girlfriend is **English**.

783- Un échange – *An exchange/A trade*

Serais-tu intéressé à faire **un échange**?
Would you be interested in making **an exchange**?

784- Un feu – *A fire*

Les pompiers sont arrivés à temps pour éteindre **le feu**.
The firemen arrived in time to put out **the fire**.

785- Satisfaire – *To satisfy*

Elle se plaint constamment, je ne sais pas quoi faire pour la **satisfaire**.
She's always complaining, I don't know what to do **to satisfy** her.

786- Observer – *To observe/To watch*

Nous allons au parc pour **observer** les oiseaux.
We are going to the park **to watch** the birds.

787- Une capacité – *A capacity*

Ce canapé a **une capacité** de poids de neuf cents livres.
This sofa has a weight **capacity** of nine hundred pounds.

788- Désigner – *To designate*

Ian veut que nous **désignions** un nouveau chef d'équipe.
Ian wants us **to designate** a new team leader.

789- Dépendre – *To depend*

Je ne sais pas si je vais venir, ça **dépend** comment je me sens.
I don't know if I'm going to come, it **depends** on how I'm feeling.

790- Neuf – *Nine*

Préparez-vous, la cloche sonne dans **neuf** secondes.
Get ready, the bell rings in **nine** seconds.

791- Construire – *To build*

Ils vont **construire** un nouveau stationnement sur ma rue.
They're going **to build** a new parking lot on my street.

792- Une scène – *A scene*

Arrête de parler, c'est ma **scène** préférée!
Stop talking, this is my favorite **scene**!

793- Durant – *During*

Je me suis endormie **durant** la messe de ce matin.
I fell asleep **during** this morning's service.

794- Un secret – *A secret*

Approche-toi, j'ai **un secret** à te dire.
Come closer, I have **a secret** to tell you.

795- Un plaisir – *A pleasure*

Ne me remerciez pas, ce fut **un plaisir**.
Don't thank me, it was **a pleasure**.

796- Un message – *A message*

J'ai **un message** pour toi de la part de ton père.
I have **a message** for you from your father.

797- Une proposition – *A proposal*

Mon patron m'a fait **une proposition** intéressante cet après-midi.
My boss made me an interesting **proposal** this afternoon.

798- Combien – *How much/How many*

Combien coûte ce bracelet?
How much is this bracelet?

799- Un dossier – *A record*

Le propriétaire ne sait pas qu'elle a **un dossier** criminel.
The owner does not know that she has a criminal **record**.

800- Une absence – *An absence*

Son **absence** me rend folle, je déteste être seule.
His **absence** is driving me crazy, I hate to be alone.

801- Cher|Chère – *Expensive*

J'aimerais acheter cette voiture, mais elle est trop **chère**.
I would love to buy this car, but it's too **expensive**.

802- Plaire – *To please*

J'ai tout essayé pour lui **plaire**.
I tried everything **to please** her.

803- Derrière – *Behind*

La prise électrique est située **derrière** l'appareil.
The electrical outlet is situated **behind** the device.

804- Une connaissance – *Knowledge*

Josée a beaucoup de **connaissances** sur le sujet, demande-lui.
Josée has a lot of **knowledge** on the subject, ask her.

805- Nul|Nulle – *Nil/Null*

Mes chances de me marier avant vingt-cinq ans sont **nulles**.
My chances to get married before I'm twenty-five are **nil**.

806- Une entrée – *An entrance*

Rejoins-moi près de **l'entrée** vers six heures.
Meet me by **the entrance** around six o'clock.

807- Signer – *To sign*

J'aimerais lire le contrat avant de le **signer**.
I would like to read the contract before **signing** it.

808- Révéler – *To reveal*

Je ne peux pas **révéler** mes secrets les plus profonds.
I can't **reveal** my deepest secrets.

809- Couper – *To cut*

Peux-tu m'aider à **couper** les légumes?
Can you help me **cut** the vegetables?

810- Une salle – *A room*

Nous avons réservé **une salle** pour ta fête d'anniversaire.
We reserved **a room** for your birthday party.

811- Immédiatement – *Immediately*

Tu dois appeler ton père **immédiatement**.
You must call your father **immediately**.

812- Une équipe – *A team*

Yves et moi faisions partie de la même **équipe** de soccer.
Yves and I were part of the same soccer **team**.

813- Situer – *To situate*

L'église est **située** sur la rue principale.
The church is **situated** on the main street.

814- Souligner – *To underline*

Soulignez tous les pronoms dans la phrase suivante.
Underline every pronoun in the following sentence.

815- Une source – *A source*

Il est important de toujours citer tes **sources**.
It's important to always quote your **sources**.

816- Une pièce – *A piece/A room*

Ce tapis sera **une pièce** centrale dans n'importe quelle **pièce** de votre maison.
This rug will be a central **piece** in any **room** of your house.

817- Un crime – *A crime*

Tu as commis **un crime**, maintenant tu dois faire face aux conséquences.
You committed **a crime**, now you must face the consequences.

818- Précédent|Précédente – *Previous*

Les consignes sont écrites à la page **précédente**.
The instructions are written on the **previous** page.

819- Installer – *To install*

Ce jeu sera très long à **installer**.
This game will be very long **to install**.

820- Facile – *Easy*

Ce n'est pas **facile** pour moi de parler de mes sentiments.
It's not **easy** for me to talk about my feelings.

821- Augmenter – *To increase*

Cette lampe **augmentera** l'attrait moderne de votre salon.

This lamp will **increase** the modern appeal of your living room.

822- Le respect – *The respect*

Aies au moins **le respect** de me le dire en face.
At least have **the respect** to say it to my face.

823- Une impression – *An impression*

Ma première **impression** n'était pas satisfaisante.
My first **impression** was not satisfying.

824- Octobre – *October*

Nous serons en voyage pendant le mois d'**octobre**.
We will be on vacation during the month of **October**.

825- Un|Une médecin – *A doctor*

Ton frère a de la fièvre, il doit aller chez **le médecin**.
Your brother has a fever, he has to go to **the doctor**.

826- Fédéral|Fédérale – *Federal*

Je n'ai pas encore reçu mon retour d'impôt **fédéral**.
I haven't received my **federal** tax return yet.

827- La police – *The police*

Montrez-vous, ou j'appelle **la police**!
Show yourself, or I'm calling **the police**!

828- Un coût – *A cost*

Le coût de fabrication est vraiment plus bas que le prix de vente.
The manufacturing **cost** is a lot lower than the selling price.

829- Réunir – *To reunite*

Nous allons enfin nous **réunir** après cinq ans.

We will finally **reunite** after five years.

830- Un contrat – *A contract*

J'ai signé **un contrat** de confidentialité.
I signed a confidentiality **contract**.

831- Normal|Normale – *Normal*

C'est parfaitement **normal** de faire des erreurs au début.
It's perfectly **normal** to make mistakes in the beginning.

832- Une attitude – *An attitude*

Change ton **attitude** si tu veux te faire des amis.
Change your **attitude** if you want to make friends.

833- Une série – *A series*

Cette **série** romantique est captivante.
This romantic **series** is captivating.

834- Une formation – *A formation*

Je vais me coucher, j'ai **une formation** tôt demain matin.
I'm going to bed, I have **a formation** early in the morning.

835- Lever – *To raise*

Tu dois **lever** ta main avant de poser une question.
You need **to raise** your hand before you ask a question.

836- Proche – *Close*

Elliot et moi sommes très **proches**.
Elliot and I are very **close**.

837- Direct|Directe – *Direct*

Il a été tellement **direct** qu'elle a failli pleurer.

He was so **direct** that she almost cried.

838- Une faute – *A mistake*

Tu as fait **une faute** d'orthographe.
You made a spelling **mistake**.

839- Figurer – *To appear*

Cette information **figure** à la troisième page du manuel.
This information **appears** on the third page of the manual.

840- Une pratique – *A practice*

On se voit à **la pratique** demain soir!
I'll see you at **practice** tomorrow evening!

841- Finalement – *Finally*

Finalement, il l'a demandée en mariage!
Finally, he asked her to marry him!
842- Allemand | Allemande – *German*
Mon compositeur préféré est **allemand**.
My favorite composer is **German**.

843- La pression – *Pressure*

Hugo a beaucoup de **pression** au travail.
Hugo has a lot of **pressure** at work.

844- Imaginer – *To imagine*

Tu ne peux pas **imaginer** comment je me sens.
You can't **imagine** how I feel.

845- Un champ – *A field*

Mon grand-père possède une ferme et **un champ**.
My grandfather owns a farm and **a field**.

846- Un film – *A film/A movie*

Ce soir, j'ai envie de regarder **un film** avec toi.
Tonight, I want to watch **a movie** with you.

847- Une charge – *A load*

Cette **charge** est trop lourde pour mon camion.
This **load** is too heavy for my truck.

848- Envisager – *To consider*

J'**envisage** toutes les possibilités avant de prendre une décision.
I **consider** all the possibilities before making a decision.

849- Un accès – *An access*

La poignée est à l'avant pour **un accès** facile.
The knob is in the front for an easy **access**.

850- Une ressource – *A resource*

L'exploitation des **ressources** naturelles devrait être régulée.
The exploitation of natural **resources** should be regulated.

851- Monter – *To go up*

Le fils de mon frère vient d'apprendre à **monter** les escaliers.
My brother's son just learned how **to go up** the stairs.

852- Promettre – *To promise*

Je crois que je vais y être, mais je ne veux rien **promettre**.
I think I'll be there, but I don't want **to promise** anything.

853- Une motion – *A motion*

Tous ceux en faveur de cette **motion** doivent lever la main.
All those in favor of this **motion** must raise their hand.

854- Concentrer – *To concentrate*

Nous devons **concentrer** nos efforts pour réussir en tant qu'équipe.
We must **concentrate** our efforts to succeed as a team.

855- Une commune – *A commune*

Quel autobus doit-on prendre pour se rendre à **la commune**?
What bus should we take to get to **the commune**?

856- Composer – *To compose*

Mon copain m'a **composé** une chanson et elle est magnifique.
My boyfriend **composed** a song for me and it's beautiful.

857- Un chemin – *A path*

Nous sommes perdus, nous avons pris le mauvais **chemin**!
We're lost, we took the wrong **path**!

858- Une zone – *An area*

C'est **la zone** où ils ont retrouvé le corps.
This is **the area** where they found the body.

859- Une province – *A province*

Le Québec est l'une des plus belles **provinces** du Canada.
Quebec is one of the most beautiful **provinces** of Canada.

860- Une élection – *An election*

Le conseil tiendra **une élection** mardi matin.
The council will hold **an election** on Tuesday morning.

861- Exactement – *Exactly*

Ce n'est pas **exactement** ce que je voulais dire.
This is not **exactly** what I meant to say.

862- Un conflit – *A conflict*

Ses mensonges sont la cause du **conflit**.
His lies are the cause of the **conflict**.

863- Hors – *Out*

Hors de ma vue! J'en ai assez!
Out of my sight! I've had enough!

864- Une enquête – *An investigation*

Nous continuerons à chercher, **l'enquête** n'est pas terminée.
We'll keep looking, **the investigation** is not completed.

865- Un terrain – *A terrain*

Cette randonnée comprend huit kilomètres sur **un terrain** escarpé.
This hike includes eight kilometers on a steep **terrain**.

866- Mars – *March*

Je suis née en **Mars**.
I was born in **March**.

867- Tellement – *So much/So many*

Il me manque **tellement**.
I miss him **so much**.

868- Un usage – *A use*

De nos jours, les téléphones ont plusieurs **usages** différents.
Nowadays, phones have many different **uses**.

869- Demain – *Tomorrow*

Laisse-moi y penser et je te reviens **demain**.
Let me think about it and I'll get back to you **tomorrow**.

870- Hier – *Yesterday*

Nous avons passé une très belle soirée ensemble **hier**.
We spent a very nice evening together **yesterday**.

871- Confier – *To entrust with*

Nous sommes meilleurs amis, je te **confierais** ma vie.
We're best friends, I would **entrust you with** my life.

872- Remarquer – *To notice*

As-tu **remarqué** qu'elles portent le même chandail?
Have you **noticed** that they're wearing the same shirt?

873- Un égard – *A regard*

Le député doit prendre une décision à **l'égard** de ce problème.
The deputee must make a decision in **regard** to this problem.

874- Supérieur|Supérieure – *Superior*

Ce bois est de qualité **supérieure**.
This wood is of **superior** quality.

875- Un espace – *A space*

Assure-toi de laisser **un espace** entre les bureaux.
Make sure you leave **a space** between the desks.

876- Condamner – *To condemn*

Il a été **condamné** à mort pour ses crimes.
He was **condemned** to death for his crimes.

877- Capital|Capitale – *Capital*

C'est une urgence **capitale**, nous n'avons pas de temps à perdre.
It's a **capital** emergency, we have no time to lose.

878- Un lien – *A bond*

Il y a **un lien** très fort entre mon père et moi.
There is a very strong **bond** between my father and me.

879- Une voiture – *A car*

Ce n'est pas très loin, pas besoin de prendre **la voiture**.
It isn't very far, no need to take **the car**.

880- Une discussion – *A discussion*

Nous aurons **une discussion** quand tu reviendras à la maison ce soir.
We'll have **a discussion** when you come back home tonight.

881- Huit – *Eight*

Je viendrai te chercher à **huit** heures et demi.
I'll come get you at **eight** and a half.

882- Justifier – *To justify*

Ta colère ne **justifie** pas tes actions.
Your anger doesn't **justify** your actions.

883- Agent|Agente - *Agent*

J'ai un rendez-vous avec mon **agent** demain matin.
I have an appointment with my **agent** tomorrow morning.

884- Un sentiment – *A feeling*

J'ignorais qu'elle avait des **sentiments** pour moi.
I didn't know she had **feelings** for me.

885- Une tâche – *A task*

Je dois accomplir cette **tâche** par moi-même.
I must complete this **task** by myself.

886- Directement – *Directly*

Tu dois lui donner cette lettre **directement**.
You must give him this letter **directly**.

887- Limiter – *To limit*

J'ai décidé de **limiter** ma consommation d'alcool.
I decided **to limit** my alcohol consumption.

888- Raconter – *To tell*

Est-ce que je t'ai déjà **raconté** cette histoire?
Have I ever **told** you this story?

889- Décembre – *December*

Au Canada, il fait très froid en **décembre**.
In Canada, it's very cold in **December**.

890- Développer – *To develop*

Nous avons **développé** une belle amitié.
We have **developed** a beautiful friendship.

891- Honorable – *Honorable*

Ma mère est une femme **honorable**.
My mother is an **honorable** woman.

892- Un contact – *A contact*

J'essaie d'établir **un contact** visuel avec la jolie femme au bar.
I'm trying to establish visual **contact** with the pretty lady at the bar.

893- Conclure – *To conclude*

Je ne sais pas comment **conclure** ce paragraphe.
I don't know how **to conclude** this paragraph.

894- Ouvert|Ouverte – *Open*

Tu as laissé la porte de la voiture **ouverte**.
You left the car door **open**.

895- Un investissement – *An investment*

Une maison est **un investissement** à long terme.
A house is a long-term **investment**.

896- Insister – *To insist*

J'ai déjà dit non, arrête d'**insister**.
I already said no, stop **insisting**.

897- Un fruit – *A fruit*

Mon médecin m'a dit de manger au moins **un fruit** par jour.
My doctor told me to eat at least **one fruit** per day.

898- Un avantage – *An advantage*

Notre équipe a **l'avantage** sur l'équipe adverse.
Our team has **the advantage** over the opposing team.

899- Historique – *Historical*

La chute de l'Empire romain fut un grand moment **historique**.
The Fall of the Roman Empire was a great **historical** moment.

900- Probablement – *Probably*

Il n'a **probablement** pas encore reçu mon message.
He **probably** hasn't received my message yet.

901- Un voyage – *A trip*
Cet été, nous ferons **un voyage** aux Bahamas.
This summer, we'll make **a trip** to the Bahamas.

902- Sept – *Seven*

La copine de François veut avoir **sept** enfants.
François' girlfriend wants to have **seven** children.

903- Une marche – *A walk*

Allons prendre **une marche** au bord de la rivière.
Let's go take **a walk** by the river.

904- Un|Une garde – *A guard*

Il y a **un garde** de sécurité à l'entrée de la bijouterie.
There is a security **guard** at the entrance of the jewelry store.

905- Commercial|Commerciale – *Commercial*

La musique populaire est très **commerciale**.
Pop music is very **commercial**.

906- Critique – *Critical*

Sa condition est **critique**, il ne lui reste plus beaucoup de temps à vivre.
Her condition is **critical**, she doesn't have much more time to live.

907- Un ministère – *A ministry*

C'est un travail pour **le ministère** de la Défense.
This is a matter for **the Ministry** of Defence.

908- Baisser – *To lower/To turn down*

Il commence à faire chaud, peux-tu **baisser** le chauffage?
It's getting hot, can you **turn down** the heat?

909- La vérité – *The truth*

Je lui ferai confiance le jour où il dira finalement **la vérité**.

I'll trust him the day he finally tells **the truth**.

910- Une culture – *A culture*

Mes deux parents se ressemblent, même s'ils sont de **cultures** différentes.
Both my parents resemble one another, even if they're from different **cultures**.

911- Cacher – *To hide*

Tu ne peux pas me **cacher** la vérité.
You can't **hide** the truth from me.

912- Prêter – *To lend*

Peux-tu me **prêter** ton ordinateur portable pour le weekend?
Can you **lend** me your laptop for the weekend?

913- Définir – *To define*

Je ne laisserai pas cet accident me **définir**.
I won't let this accident **define** me.

914- Une somme – *A sum*

La somme de ces deux variables sera toujours constante.
The sum of these two variables will always be constant.

915- Exposer – *To display*

J'**exposerai** cette œuvre d'art dans mon salon.
I will **display** this piece of art in my living room.

916- Un progrès – *Progress*

Tu as fait beaucoup de **progrès** depuis le début de cette leçon.
You have made a lot of **progress** since the beginning of this lesson.

917- Un|Une secrétaire – *A secretary*

Veuillez laisser un message à **la secrétaire** du Dr. Raymond.
Please leave a message to Dr. Raymond's **secretary**.

918- La mer – *The sea*

Ce chien n'avait encore jamais vu **la mer**.
This dog had never seen **the sea** before.

919- Rapporter – *To bring back*

N'oublis pas de me **rapporter** mon chargeur quand tu auras fini avec.
Don't forget **to bring** me **back** my charger when you're done with it.

920- Appuyer – *To support*

Il n'a aucun argument valide pour **appuyer** sa thèse.
He has no valid argument **to support** his thesis.

921- Client|Cliente – *Client*

Le client n'est pas satisfait, il veut se faire rembourser.
The client is not satisfied, he wants his money back.

922- Rentrer – *To come back*

Suzanne est **rentrée** tôt hier soir; la fête était ennuyeuse.
Suzanne **came back** early last night; the party was boring.

923- Une mémoire – *A memory*

J'ai une excellente **mémoire**, je me rappelle de tout.
I have an excellent **memory**, I remember everything.

924- Un caractère – *A character*

Ton chat a un très mauvais **caractère**.
Your cat has a very bad **character**.

925- Détruire – *To destroy*

Leur divorce va **détruire** la vie de leurs enfants.
Their divorce is going **to destroy** their children's lives.

926- Civil|Civile – *Civil*

Le recyclage est la responsabilité **civile** de tous.
Recycling is everyone's **civil** responsibility.

927- Une liste – *A list*

J'ai fait **une liste** de toutes les choses que je dois acheter pour la fête.
I made **a list** of all the things I have to buy for the party.

928- Juin – *June*

Annabelle se Marie le vingt-six **juin**.
Annabelle is getting married **June** twenty-sixth.

929- Un danger – *A danger*

Cet homme est **un danger** au volant.
This man is **a danger** behind the wheel.

930- Complexe – *Complex*

Cette sculpture m'impressionne avec tous ses détails **complexes**.
This sculpture impresses me with all its **complex** details.

931- Un commerce – *A trade*

Notre pays encourage **le commerce** libre et équitable.
Our country encourages free and fair **trade**.

932- Le transport – *Transportation*

Pour l'instant, son vélo est son seul moyen de **transport**.
For now, his bicycle is his only means of **transportation**.

933- Une nécessité – *A necessity*

Tu n'avais pas besoin d'acheter cette robe, ce n'était pas **une nécessité**.
You didn't need to buy this dress, it wasn't **a necessity**.

934- Une institution – *An institution*

Mon oncle travaille pour **une institution** indépendante.
My uncle works for an independent **institution**.

935- Une défense – *A defense*

Pour ma **défense**, il était déjà trop tard pour faire quoi que ce soit.
In my **defense**, it was already too late to do anything.

936- Janvier – *January*

À Montréal, **janvier** est normalement le mois le plus froid.
In Montreal, **January** is normally the coldest month.

937- S'échapper – *To escape*

Il est impossible de **s'échapper** de cette prison.
It's impossible **to escape** from this prison.

938- Une négociation – *A negotiation*

Va mettre la table immédiatement, ce n'est pas **une négociation**.
Go set the table immediately, this isn't **a negotiation**.

939- Une attente – *A wait*

Comment est **l'attente** à la clinique ce matin?
How's **the wait** at the clinic this morning?

940- Mai – *May*

Mon dernier examen est le dix-huit **mai**.
My last exam is on **May** eighteenth.

941- Septembre – *September*

Nous serons aux États-Unis pendant tout le mois de **septembre**.
We will be in the United States during the entire month of
September.

942- Un environnement – *An environment*

Tout le monde doit lutter pour **l'environnement** à sa propre
manière.
Everyone needs to fight for **the environment** in his own way.

943- Séparer – *To separate*

La partie du bas est facile à **séparer** du reste.
The bottom part is easy **to separate** from the rest.

944- Une réaction – *A reaction*

Explique-toi, parce que je ne comprends pas ta **réaction**.
Explain yourself, because I don't understand your **reaction**.

945- Franc|Franche – *Frank*

J'ai besoin d'une femme qui n'a pas peur d'être **franche**.
I need a woman that's not afraid to be **frank**.

946- Positif|Positive – *Positive*

Les résultats du test étaient **positifs**.
The test results were **positive**.

947- Scientifique – *Scientific*

N'interromps pas mon expérience **scientifique**!
Don't interrupt my **scientific** experiment!

948- Un papier – *A paper*

Elle m'a écrit une lettre sur du **papier** de soie.

She wrote me a letter on silk **paper**.

949- Une expression – *An expression*

Ne le prends pas au sens littéral, ce n'était qu'**une expression**.
Don't take it in the literal sense, it was only **an expression**.

950- Une disposition – *A disposition*

La disposition de cette lampe change complètement le décor.
The disposition of this lamp completely changes the décor.

951- Indépendant|Indépendante – *Independent*

J'ai beaucoup aimé ce film **indépendant**.
I really enjoyed this **independent** movie.

952- Une carte – *A card*

Lis **la carte** avant de déballer le cadeau.
Read **the card** before you unwrap the present.

953- Une association – *An association*

Jean est le directeur d'**une association** américaine.
Jean is the director of an American **association**.

954- Régler – *To fix*

Je ne peux pas **régler** tes problèmes pour toi.
I can't **fix** your problems for you.

955- Un modèle – *A model*

Je préfère **le modèle** de la série A.
I prefer **the model** from the A-series.

956- Une protection – *Protection*

Ce cadenas offre **une protection** assurée contre le vol.

This padlock offers a guaranteed **protection** against theft.

957- Étudier – *To study*

Je ne peux pas **étudier** avec tout ce bruit.
I can't **study** with all this noise.

958- Déterminer – *To determine*

Ont-ils **déterminé** la cause du décès?
Have they **determined** the cause of death?

959- Un budget – *A budget*

Mon **budget** ne me permet pas de sortir ce soir.
My **budget** doesn't allow me to go out tonight.

960- Fonder – *To found*

Cette entreprise a été **fondée** en 1948.
This company was **founded** in 1948.

961- Une structure – *A structure*

La structure en acier inoxydable est très solide.
The stainless-steel **structure** is very solid.

962- Commander – *To order*

J'ai envie de **commander** de la pizza ce soir.
I feel like **ordering** pizza tonight.

963- Exercer – *To exercise (something)*

Je suis assez vieille pour **exercer** le droit de voter.
I'm old enough **to exercise** the right to vote.

964- Un amour – *A love*

C'était **l'amour** au premier regard.

It was **love** at first sight.

965- Manifester – *To show*

Elle n'a **manifesté** aucun intérêt envers moi.
She has **shown** no interest towards me.

966- Menacer – *To threaten*

Son père a **menacé** de le mettre à la porte.
His father **threatened** to kick him out.

967- Conseiller – *To advise*

J'ai besoin plus d'informations pour mieux vous **conseiller**.
I need more information to better **advise** you.

968- Complet|Complète – *Full/Complete*

Désolé, nous sommes **complet**. Revenez demain.
Sorry, we're **full**. Come back tomorrow.

969- Une opposition – *Opposition*

Ton déni représente **une opposition** envers tout ce en quoi je crois.
Your denial represents **opposition** towards everything I believe in.

970- Une maladie – *A disease*

Le médecin a dit que ce n'était pas **une maladie** contagieuse.
The doctor said it wasn't a contagious **disease**.

971- En outre – *Besides*

En outre, il y aura de la pluie mardi matin.
Besides, there will be rain on Tuesday morning.

972- Tandis que – *While*

J'irai au supermarché **tandis que** Pierre sera dans la douche.
I will go to the supermarket **while** Pierre will be in the shower.

973- La construction – *The construction*

La construction en bois de cette table la rend durable.
The wood **construction** of this table makes it durable.

974- Une bande – *A strip*

La bande d'acier tourne dans le sens horaire.
The iron **strip** rotates clockwise.

975- Un signal – *A signal*

Attends **le signal** avant de commencer à courir.
Wait for **the signal** before you start running.

976- Une réunion – *A meeting*

Je ne peux pas répondre au téléphone pendant ma **réunion**.
I can't answer the phone during my **meeting**.

977- Une réforme – *A reform*

Beaucoup ne sont pas satisfaits de **la réforme** de l'orthographe.
Many are not satisfied with the spelling **reform**.

978- Rejeter – *To reject*

Réfléchis avant de **rejeter** mon idée.
Think before you **reject** my idea.

979- Novembre – *November*

Ce groupe sera en tournée pendant tout le mois de **novembre**.
This band will be on tour during the entire month of **November**.

980- Un fonds – *A fund*

Nous avons créé **un fonds** pour financer notre nouveau projet.
We created **a fund** to finance our new project.

981- Coûter – *To cost*

Je n'ai pas beaucoup d'argent, j'espère que ça ne va pas **coûter**
trop cher.
I don't have a lot of money, I hope it won't **cost** too much.

982- Voisin|Voisine – *Neighbor*

Parfois, je prends le thé avec ma **voisine**.
Sometimes, I have tea with my **neighbor**.

983- La presse – *The press*

Cette information ne peut pas tomber entre les mains de **la presse**.
This information can't fall into the hands of **the press**.

984- Rouge – *Red*

As-tu vu ma robe **rouge**? Je ne la trouve pas.
Have you seen my **red** dress? I can't find it.

985- La majorité – *The majority*

La majorité a voté pour le même candidat que l'an dernier.
The majority voted for the same candidate as last year.

986- Autoriser – *To authorize*

J'ai besoin de votre signature pour **autoriser** le paiement.
I need your signature **to authorize** the payment.

987- Effectuer – *To carry out*

Crois-tu que tu pourras **effectuer** ce travail à temps?
Do you think you can **carry out** this work in time?

988- Une reprise – *A resumption*

Soyez de retour dans quinze minutes pour **la reprise** du cours.
Be back in fifteen minutes for **the resumption** of the class.

989- Central|Centrale – *Central*

Ce chandelier est la pièce **centrale** de la chambre.
This candlestick is the **central** piece of the room.

990- Une procédure – *A procedure*

Je vais maintenant vous expliquer **la procédure**.
I will now explain to you **the procedure**.

991- Une faveur – *A favor*

J'ai **une faveur** à te demander.
I have **a favor** to ask you.

992- Une éducation – *An education*

Ton **éducation** est ce qu'il y a de plus important en ce moment.
Your **education** is what's most important at the moment.

993- Officiel|Officielle – *Official*

Ce document porte le sceau **officiel** de l'Université.
This document bears the **official** seal of the University.

994- Un document – *A document*

Vous devez m'apporter ce **document** avant demain.
You must bring me this **document** before tomorrow.

995- Le bord – *The edge*

Ne mange pas si près du **bord** de la table.
Don't eat so close to **the edge** of the table.

996- Retourner – *To return/To go back*

J'ai adoré le Mexique, j'ai hâte d'y **retourner**!
I loved Mexico, I can't wait **to go back** there!

997- Professionnel|Professionnelle – *Professional*

Ce genre de comportement n'est pas **professionnel**.
This kind of behavior is not **professional**.

998- Un aspect – *An aspect*

Nous n'avons pas eu le temps de parler de tous les **aspects** du projet.
We didn't have time to talk about all the **aspects** of the project.

999- Un animal – *An animal*

Le guépard est **un animal** gracieux.
The cheetah is a graceful **animal**.

1000- Utile – *Useful*

Ce tournevis est très **utile**.
This screwdriver is very **useful**.

1001- S'inscrire – *To register/To apply*

Je veux **m'inscrire** à un programme d'arts.
I want **to apply** to an arts program.

1002- La concurrence – *The competition*

Nos produits sont plus fiables que ceux de **la concurrence**.
Our products are more reliable than those from **the competition**.

1003- Une déclaration – *A declaration*

Il a fait sa **déclaration** devant tout le monde.
He made his **declaration** in front of everybody.

1004- Auparavant – *Beforehand*

Je ne l'avais pas rencontrée **auparavant**.
I had not met her **beforehand**.

1005- Mille – *One thousand*

Elle a dû t'aider au moins **mille** fois.
She must have helped you at least **a thousand** times.

1006- Absolument – *Absolutely*

Je ne veux **absolument** pas y aller.
I **absolutely** don't want to go.

1007- Une prison – *A prison*

Cette école est comme **une prison**.
This school is like **a prison**.

1008- Une armée – *An army*

Plusieurs de mes amis sont dans **l'armée**.
Many of my friends are in **the army**.

1009- Rejoindre – *To join*

À quelle heure viendras-tu nous **rejoindre**?
At what time will you come **join** us?

1010- Complètement – *Completely*

Je refuse, cette idée est **complètement** inappropriée.
I refuse, this idea is **completely** inappropriate.

1011- Confirmer – *To confirm*

N'oublis pas de **confirmer** ta présence.
Don't forget **to confirm** your presence.

1012- Un salaire – *A salary*

Le salaire de ma femme est plus élevé que le mien.
My wife's **salary** is higher than mine.

1013- Une lecture – *A reading*

Je ferai **une lecture** de ce livre devant la classe demain.
I will do **a reading** of this book in front of the class tomorrow.

1014- Un revenu – *A revenue*

Ce métier est épuisant, mais il permet **un revenu** élevé.
This job is exhausting, but it allows for a high **revenue**.

1015- Attaquer – *To attack*

Vanessa s'est faite **attaquer** devant chez elle hier soir.
Vanessa was **attacked** in front of her house last night.

1016- Une table – *A table*

Je viens d'acheter une nouvelle **table** d'appoint pour le salon.
I just bought a new side **table** for the living room.

1017- Remonter – *To go back up*

Je n'ai pas envie de **remonter** les escaliers, prenons l'ascenceur.
I don't feel like **going back up** the stairs, let's take the elevator.

1018- Certes – *Certainly*

Certes, il aura beaucoup de travail à faire s'il veut être promu.
Certainly, he will have a lot of work to do if he wants to be promoted.

1019- Contribuer – *To contribute*

J'apprécie beaucoup que tu **contribues** au projet.
I really appreciate that you're **contributing** to the project.

1020- Autrement – *Differently*

À ta place, je ferais les choses **autrement**.
In your place, I would do things **differently**.

1021- Ferme – *Firm*

Je déteste dormir sur un matelas qui soit trop **ferme**.
I hate to sleep on a mattress that's too **firm**.

1022- Désormais – *From now on*

Désormais, je veux que tu m'appelles à dix-neuf heures tous les jours.
From now on, I want you to call me at seven everyday.

1023- Lourd|Lourde – *Heavy*

J'ai besoin d'aide, c'est trop **lourd** pour moi.
I need help, it's too **heavy** for me.

1024- Susciter – *To generate*

Son travail a **suscité** l'intérêt des professionnels.
His work has **generated** interest from the professionals.

1025- Avril – *April*

Ma mère revient de son voyage en **avril**.
My mother returns from her vacation in **April**.

1026- Dur|Dure – *Hard*

C'est très **dur** pour moi de me concentrer en classe.
It's very **hard** for me to concentrate in class.

1027- Une application – *An application*

Je n'ai pas encore reçu ton **application**.
I still haven't received your **application**.

1028- Lutter – *To struggle*

Sa mère **lutte** contre la maladie mentale.
Her mother **struggles** with mental issues.

1029- Un profit – *A profit*

Ce projet générera beaucoup de **profits**.
This project will generate a lot of **profits**.

1030- Contenir – *To contain*

Cette boîte **contient** tous mes souvenirs d'enfance.
This box **contains** all of my childhood memories.

1031- Une république – *A republic*

Ma grand-mère a quitté **la république** il y a longtemps.
My grandmother left **the republic** a long time ago.

1032- Déposer – *To put down*

Dépose l'argent sur la table et va-t-en.
Put the money **down** on the table and go.

1033- La communication – *Communication*

La communication est la clé d'une relation saine.
Communication is the key to a healthy relationship.

1034- Un jugement – *A judgement*

Cette décision était une erreur de **jugement**.
This decision was an error of **judgement**.

1035- Un manque – *A lack*

Il y a **un manque** de sel dans cette sauce.
There is **a lack** of salt in this sauce.

1036- Modifier – *To modify*

Elle a **modifié** sa signature.
She **modified** her signature.

1037- Traverser – *To cross*

Nous allons **traverser** la rivière à la nage.
We are going **to cross** the river by swimming.

1038- Transformer – *To transform*

Cette chenille va bientôt se **transformer** en papillon.
This caterpillar will soon **transform** into a butterfly.

1039- Un engagement – *A commitment*

Tu dois respecter ton **engagement**.
You need to respect your **commitment**.

1040- Un frère – *A brother*

Le frère de Guillaume a une très belle voiture.
Guillaume's **brother** has a very nice car.

1041- Mardi – *Tuesday*

Je vais t'appeler **mardi** matin.
I'm going to call you on **Tuesday** morning.

1042- Un échec – *A failure*

Cet **échec** va seulement te rendre plus fort.
This **failure** will only make you stronger.

1043- Un vote – *A vote*

Ce candidat n'aura pas mon **vote**.
This candidate won't have my **vote**.

1044- Renvoyer – *To send back*

Je ne crois pas que tu aies reçu mon message, je vais te le **renvoyer**.
I don't think that you received my message, I'm going to **send** it **back** to you.

1045- Regretter – *To regret*

J'ai vécu une belle vie, je n'ai rien à **regretter**.
I lived a beautiful life, I have nothing **to regret**.

1046- Une espèce – *A species*

Le gorille est **une espèce** en voie de disparition.
The gorilla is an endangered **species**.

1047- Une recommandation – *A recommendation*

Laisse-moi te faire **une recommandation**.
Let me give you **a recommendation**.

1048- Consister – *To consist*

Ce projet **consiste** en trois étapes faciles.
This project **consists** of three easy steps.

1049- Une rencontre – *A meeting*

J'ai **une rencontre** avec mon nouveau patron à midi.
I have **a meeting** with my new boss at twelve.

1050- Surprendre – *To surprise*

J'ai tout essayé pour la **surprendre**, rien ne fonctionne.
I tried everything **to surprise** her, nothing works.

1051- Une circonstance – *A circumstance*

J'aurais voulu te rencontrer dans des **circonstances** différentes.

I would have liked to meet you under different **circumstances**.

1052- Un|Une témoin – *A witness*

La police a questionné **le témoin** de l'accident.
The police questioned **the witness** of the accident.

1053- Améliorer – *To improve*

Connaître le vocabulaire est essentiel pour **améliorer** ton français.
Knowing the vocabulary is essential **to improve** your French.

1054- Une administration – *Administration*

Laissez-moi rediriger votre appel au bureau de **l'administration**.
Let me redirect your call to the **administration** office.

1055- Réagir – *To react*

Je ne sais pas comment Rémi va **réagir** à la nouvelle.
I don't know how Rémi is going **to react** to the news.

1056- Une lumière – *A light*

J'ai besoin d'un peu plus de **lumière** pour lire.
I need a little bit more **light** to read.

1057- Vert|Verte – *Green*

La lumière est **verte**, on peut y aller maintenant.
The light is **green**, we can go now.

1058- Apprécier – *To appreciate*

J'**apprécie** vraiment tout ce que tu as fait pour moi.
I really **appreciate** everything you've done for me.

1059- Un combat – *A fight*

On va au bar pour regarder **le combat** à la télé.

We're going to the bar to watch **the fight** on TV.

1060- Sensible – *Sensitive*

Il pleure tout le temps, il est beaucoup trop **sensible**.
He cries all the time, he is far too **sensitive**.

1061- Étudiant|Étudiante – *Student*

Ma tante est encore **étudiante**, elle adore apprendre de nouvelles choses.
My aunt is still a **student**, she loves to learn new things.

1062- Réfléchir – *To reflect*

J'ai besoin de temps pour **réfléchir** à ton commentaire.
I need some time **to reflect** on your comment.

1063- Malade – *Sick*

Je suis **malade** depuis deux semaines.
I have been **sick** for two weeks.

1064- Une portée – *A reach*

La portée de cette entreprise s'étend sur l'ensemble du marché.
This company's **reach** extends over the entire market.

1065- Un|Une élève – *A student*

J'ai vingt-six **élèves** dans ma classe.
I have twenty-six **students** in my class.

1066- Contrôler – *To control*

Tu ne peux pas **contrôler** ses actions, laisse-la faire son travail.
You can't **control** her actions, let her do her job.

1067- Merci – *Thank you*

Merci beaucoup d'être venus ce soir.
Thank you so much for coming tonight.

1068- Une vitesse – *A speed*

Il a franchi la ligne d'arrivée à **une vitesse** incroyable.
He crossed the finish line at an incredible **speed**.

1069- Une visite – *A visit*

Je vous remercie de votre **visite**, revenez bientôt!
I thank you for your **visit**, come back soon!

1070- Une assemblée – *An assembly*

Elle a présenté son projet devant **l'assemblée**.
She presented her project in front of **the assembly**.

1071- Une émission – *An emission*

Ce produit aide à réduire **l'émission** de gaz à effet de serre.
This product helps decrease **the emission** of greenhouse gas.

1072- Une arrivée – *An arrival*

J'attends ton **arrivée** depuis un mois.
I have been waiting for your **arrival** for a month.

1073- Une puissance – *A power*

J'ai besoin de plus de **puissance** pour démarrer la batterie.
I need more **power** to start the battery.

1074- Certainement – *Certainly*

Je ne lui prêterai **certainement** pas ma voiture.
I **certainly** won't lend her my car.

1075- Contenter – *To satisfy*

C'est très difficile de le **contenter**.
It's very difficult **to satisfy** him.

1076- Une perte – *A loss*

Ne pleure pas à cause de cette **perte**, tout ira mieux demain.
Don't cry over this **loss**, everything will be better tomorrow.

1077- Libéral|Libérale – *Liberal*

Yvon a voté pour le gouvernement **libéral**.
Yvon voted for the **Liberal** government.

1078- Citoyen|Citoyenne – *Citizen*

Je vis aux États-Unis, mais je suis aussi une **citoyenne** canadienne.
I live in the United States, but I am also a Canadian **citizen**.

1079- Citer – *To cite/To quote*

J'ai fini ma dissertation, je dois maintenant **citer** mes sources.
I finished my essay, I now need **to cite** my sources.

1080- Un|Une partenaire – *A partner*

Vous aurez besoin d'**un partenaire** pour faire ce travail.
You will need **a partner** to do this job.

1081- Un camp – *A camp*

Ma fille passera l'été au **camp** musical.
My daughter will spend the summer at music **camp**.

1082- Un établissement – *An institution/An establishment*

L'**établissement** de la loi 101 a été réalisé dans cet **établissement**.
The establishment of Bill 101 was conducted in this **institution**.

1083- Vendredi – *Friday*

Vendredi est mon jour de congé.
Friday is my day off.

1084- Une avance – *An advance*

J'ai besoin d'**une avance**; peux-tu me payer aujourd'hui?
I need **an advance**; can you pay me today?

1085- Destiner – *To intend*

Cet ensemble de patio est **destiné** pour une utilisation à l'extérieur.
This patio set is **intended** for an outdoors use.

1086- Une influence – *An influence*

Cette musique a une mauvaise **influence** sur ton comportement.
This music has a bad **influence** on your behavior.

1087- Nord – *North*

J'habite au **nord** du pays.
I live in the **North** of the country.

1088- Lundi – *Monday*

Qu'est-ce que tu fais **lundi**?
What are you doing on **Monday**?

1089- Un maître – *A master*

William est un **maître** de la cuisine.
William is **a master** of cooking.

1090- Interroger – *To interrogate*

La cour est sur le point d'**interroger** l'accusé.
The court is about **to interrogate** the accused.

1091- Une conférence – *A conference*

Je suis allée à **une conférence** très intéressante ce weekend.
I went to a very interesting **conference** this weekend.

1092- Causer – *To cause*

Qu'est-ce qui aurait pu **causer** autant de dommage?
What could have **caused** so much damage?

1093- Une vente – *A sale*

Cette robe est en **vente**, je crois que je vais l'acheter.
This dress is on **sale**, I think I'm going to buy it.

1094- Ramener – *To bring back*

Pourrais-tu me **ramener** le marteau que je t'ai prêté?
Could you **bring** me **back** the hammer I lent you?

1095- Soldat|Soldate – *Soldier*

Ce **soldat** mérite la médaille d'honneur.
This **soldier** deserves the medal of honor.

1096- Un|Une collègue – *A colleague*

Laurence est **la collègue** de travail avec laquelle je m'entends le mieux.
Laurence is the work **colleague** I get along with the most.

1097- Provoquer – *To provoke*

Arrête de me **provoquer** si tu ne veux pas que je me fâche.
Stop **provoking** me if you don't want me to get angry.

1098- Concevoir – *To conceive*

Il est difficile de **concevoir** une telle chose, je suis impressionné.
It's hard **to conceive** such a thing, I'm impressed.

1099- Un poids – *A weight*

Ce **poids** est trop lourd pour moi.
This **weight** is too heavy for me.

1100- Voici – *This is*

Voici ma voisine Carole.
This is my neighbor Carole.

1101- Acquérir – *To acquire*

Elle a **acquis** de nombreux talents grâce à ses études.
She **acquired** many skills thanks to her studies.

1102- Le|La moindre – *The slightest*

Je n'en ai pas **la moindre** idée.
I don't have **the slightest** idea.

1103- Convenir – *To be suitable*

Ta tenue ne **conviendra** pas pour le dîner de ce soir.
Your outfit won't **be suitable** for tonight's dinner.

1104- Procéder – *To proceed*

Il y a deux différentes manières de **procéder**.
There are two different ways **to proceed**.

1105- Examiner – *To examine*

Le médecin est prêt à **examiner** le corps de la victime.
The doctor is ready **to examine** the victim's body.

1106- Un soin – *A care*

Ne t'en fais pas, je vais bien prendre **soin** de toi.
Don't worry, I'll take good **care** of you.

1107- Mesurer – *To measure*

Mon amour pour toi ne peut pas être **mesuré**.
My love for you cannot be **measured**.

1108- Un traitement – *A treatment*

Le traitement des données prendra huit heures.
The treatment of the data will take eight hours.

1109- Jeudi – *Thursday*

Je finis de travailler tôt ce **jeudi**.
I get off work early this **Thursday**.

1110- Impliquer – *To imply/To implicate*

Cela **implique** que Marie était **impliquée** sans le savoir.
This **implies** that Marie was **implicated** without her knowledge.

1111- Une logique – *Logic*

La logique peut vous aider à résoudre ce problème mathématique.
Logic can help you solve this mathematical problem.

1112- Un individu – *An individual*

Chaque **individu** est libre de faire ses propres choix.
Each **individual** is free to make his or her own choices.

1113- Une donnée – *A datum*

Je n'ai pas eu le temps de sauvegarder mes **données**!
I didn't have time to save my **data**!

1114- Demi|Demie – *Half*

Rejoins-moi à l'aéroport dans une heure et **demie**.

Meet me at the airport in one hour and a **half**.

1115- Combattre – *To fight*

George a créé un organisme pour **combattre** la pauvreté dans son quartier.
George has created an organism **to fight** poverty in his neighborhood.

1116- Violent|Violente – *Violent*

Francis devient **violent** quand il boit.
Francis becomes **violent** when he drinks.

1117- Une science – *A science*

Ce n'est pas **une science** exacte, mais ça devrait marcher.
This is not an exact **science**, but it should work.

1118- Suivant|Suivante – *Next*

Benoît est **le suivant**, ensuite c'est ton tour.
Benoît is **next**, then it's your turn.

1119- Mériter – *To deserve*

Tu as eu ce que tu **méritais**.
You got what you **deserved**.

1120- Emprunter – *To borrow*

Est-ce que je peux **emprunter** la voiture ce soir?
Can I **borrow** the car tonight?

1121- Une conscience – *A conscience*

Anne n'a aucune **conscience** sociale.
Anne has no social **conscience**.

1122- Comporter – *To comprise of*

L'ensemble **comporte** une table et quatre chaises.
The set **comprises of** a table and four chairs.

1123- Le sang – *The blood*

Il y a un taux élevé de glucose dans son **sang**.
There is a high level of glucose in her **blood**.

1124- Un millier – *A thousand*

Il devait y avoir au moins **un millier** de personnes.
There had to be at least **a thousand** people.

1125- Emporter – *To carry away*

Tu vas te faire **emporter** par le courant.
You are going to get **carried away** by the current.

1126- Une initiative – *An initiative*

C'était une bonne **initiative** de sa part.
It was a good **initiative** on her part.

1127- Nucléaire – *Nuclear*

Les armes **nucléaires** n'auraient jamais dûes être inventées.
Nuclear weapons should have never been invented.

1128- Traduire – *To translate*

J'ai besoin de ton aide pour **traduire** ce paragraphe.
I need your help **to translate** this paragraph.

1129- Vif|Vive – *Lively*

Les couleurs **vives** de ce tapis attireront définitivement l'attention.
The **lively** colors of this rug will definitely draw attention.

1130- Exact|Exacte – *Exact*

Rejoins-moi à cet endroit **exact**.
Meet me at this **exact** spot.

1131- Une exception – *An exception*

Êtes-vous sûr de ne pas pouvoir faire **une exception**?
Are you sure you can't make **an exception**?

1132- Doubler – *To double*

Ça y est, je **double** ma mise!
That's it, I **double** my wager!

1133- Février – *February*

Il fait encore très froid en **février**.
It's still very cold in **February**.

1134- Un mode – *A mode*

Mets ton téléphone en **mode** avion.
Put your phone in airplane **mode**.

1135- Industriel|Industrielle – *Industrial*

Yannick adore la musique **industrielle**.
Yannick loves **industrial** music.

1136- La musique – *The music*

Je ne sais pas ce que je ferais sans **musique**.
I don't know what I'd do withtout **music**.

1137- La gestion – *Management*

Xavier étudie la **gestion** financière.
Xavier is studying financial **management**.

1138- Un honneur – *An honor*

Ce serait un véritable **honneur** pour moi de t'accompagner.
It would be a true **honor** for me to accompany you.

1139- Vaste – *Vast*

Mon arrière-grand-père possédait une **vaste** terre.
My great-grandfather owned a **vast** land.

1140- Évoquer – *To evoke*

Ce film a **évoqué** beaucoup de mauvais souvenirs.
This movie has **evoked** many bad memories.

1141- Tendre – *To stretch*

Nous allons devoir **tendre** la corde encore plus que ça.
We'll have **to stretch** the rope even more than that.

1142- Une étape – *A step*

Tu dois suivre les **étapes** dans l'ordre.
You must follow the **steps** in order.

1143- Physique – *Physical*

La douleur n'est pas seulement psychologique, elle est aussi **physique**.
The pain is not only psychological, it's also **physical**.

1144- Accuser – *To accuse*

Tu ne peux pas m'**accuser** sans preuve.
You can't **accuse** me without proof.

1145- Parfaitement – *Perfectly*

Ma voiture fonctionne **parfaitement** depuis que le mécanicien l'a réparée.

My car works **perfectly** since the mechanic repaired it.

1146- Une méthode – *A method*

Quelle **méthode** as-tu utilisée pour accomplir cette tâche?
What **method** did you use to accomplish this task?

1147- Fonctionner – *To work*

J'ai besoin d'aide, mon ordinateur ne **fonctionne** plus.
I need help, my computer doesn't **work** anymore.

1148- Envers – *Towards*

Ton attitude **envers** moi est inacceptable.
Your attitude **towards** me is unacceptable.

1149- Distribuer – *To distribute*

Cette entreprise **distribue** des produits à travers le monde entier.
This company **distributes** products throughout the entire world.

1150- Une existence – *An existence*

Je n'avais jamais entendu parler de son **existence**.
I had never heard of its **existence**.

1151- Prétendre – *To pretend*

Il **prétend** être quelqu'un d'autre et c'est pathétique.
He **pretends** to be someone else and it's pathetic.

1152- Global|Globale – *Global*

Cette couleur augmente l'attrait **global** de la pièce.
This color increases the **global** appeal of the room.

1153- Un|Une professeur – *A professor*

Il faut de nombreuses années d'études pour devenir **professeur**.

It takes numerous years of schooling to become a **professor**.

1154- Le crédit – *The credit*

Le gagnant aura **le crédit** qu'il mérite.
The winner will have **the credit** he deserves.

1155- Une tendance – *A tendency*

Martine a **tendance** à conduire trop vite.
Martine has **a tendency** to drive too fast.

1156- Une chaîne – *A chain*

Il m'a acheté **une chaîne** en or délicate pour mon anniversaire.
He bought me a delicate gold **chain** for my birthday.

1157- Un dommage – *Damage*

Tu devras certainement payer pour **les dommages**.
You will certainly have to pay for **the damages**.

1158- Une note – *A note/A grade*

J'ai écrit **une note** au bas de la page qui explique comment vos **notes** ont été calculées.
I wrote **a note** at the bottom of the page that explains how your **grades** were calculated.

1159- Une réserve – *A reserve*

Ceci est une bouteille de ma **réserve** personnelle.
This is a bottle from my personal **reserve**.

1160- Le maximum – *The maximum*

Choisis l'option qui offre **le maximum** d'avantages.
Choose the option that offers **maximum** advantage.

1161- Un moteur – *A motor*

Il a installé **un moteur** sur sa bicyclette; ça a l'air amusant.
He installed **a motor** on his bicycle; this looks fun.

1162- Une version – *A version*

Envoyez-moi **la version** finale par courriel.
Send me the final **version** by email.

1163- Un règlement – *A rule*

Tu n'as pas le choix, c'est **le règlement**.
You have no choice, it's **the rule**.

1164- Relatif|Relative – *Relative*

Ce principe est **relatif**, il dépend de différents facteurs.
This principle is **relative**, it depends on various factors.

1165- Mercredi – *Wednesday*

Je vais me coucher tôt **mercredi**.
I will go to bed early on **Wednesday**.

1166- Régional|Régionale – *Regional*

Notre équipe a remporté le tournoi **regional**.
Our team won the **regional** tournament.

1167- Sinon – *Otherwise*

Range ta chambre, **sinon** tu seras privé de sortie.
Clean your room, **otherwise** you'll be grounded.

1168- Entreprendre – *To undertake*

Nous devons d'abord **entreprendre** une vérification des informations.
We first need **to undertake** a verification of the information.

1169- Au-delà – *Beyond*

La beauté de cet endroit va **au-delà** de l'imaginaire.
The beauty of this place goes **beyond** imagination.

1170- S'étendre – *To lie down*

J'ai mal à la tête, je vais aller **m'étendre**.
I have a headache, I'm going to go **lie down**.

1171- Un couple – *A couple*

Ce **couple** vient au café chaque semaine.
This **couple** comes to the café every week.

1172- Profond|Profonde – *Deep*

Les paroles de cette chanson sont très **profondes**.
The lyrics of this song are very **deep**.

1173- Décrire – *To describe*

Pouvez-vous **décrire** votre agresseur?
Can you **describe** your assailant?

1174- Récent|Récente – *Recent*

Son téléphone est très **récent**, elle vient de l'acheter.
Her phone is very **recent**, she just bought it.

1175- Une télévision – *A television*

Ne t'assois pas trop près de **la télévision**.
Don't sit too close to **the television**.

1176- La retraite – *Retirement*

Quel dommage qu'il se soit blessé au dos si près de **la retraite**.
What a pity he hurt his back so close to **retirement**.

1177- Une sortie – *An exit*

Je vais venir te chercher à **la sortie**.
I'll come get you at **the exit**.

1178- Une frontière – *A border*

Je suis près de **la frontière** des États-Unis.
I am close to the United States **border**.

1179- Égal|Égale – *Equal*

Nos droits ne sont pas **égaux** à ceux de certains autres citoyens.
Our rights are not **equal** to those of some other citizens.

1180- Une promesse – *A promise*

Il m'a fait **une promesse** avant de partir.
He made me **a promise** before he left.

1181- Entretenir – *To maintain*

Je désire **entretenir** une bonne relation de travail avec mon patron.
I wish **to maintain** a good working relationship with my boss.

1182- Habiter – *To live*

Je n'aimerais pas **habiter** en ville.
I would not like **to live** in the city.

1183- Un quartier – *A district*

Je préfère habiter dans **un quartier** tranquille.
I prefer to live in a quiet **district**.

1184- Un art – *An art*

La cuisine est **un art**.

Cooking is **an art**.

1185- Accueillir – *To welcome*

Ma famille vient en visite ce weekend, j'ai hâte de les **accueillir**.
My family is coming to visit this weekend, I can't wait **to welcome** them.

1186- Libérer – *To liberate*

Libérez-moi de toute cette souffrance.
Liberate me from all this suffering.

1187- Vivant|Vivante – *Alive*

Heureusement, David était encore **vivant** après l'accident.
Fortunately, David was still **alive** after the accident.

1188- Une université – *A university*

J'assisterai à la conférence de ce professeur à **l'université**.
I will attend this professor's conference at the **university**.

1189- Rire – *To laugh*

Arrête de **rire**, je suis très sérieuse!
Stop **laughing**, I'm very serious!

1190- Avocat|Avocate – *Lawyer*

Mon fils veut devenir **avocat**, je suis si fière de lui.
My son wants to be a **lawyer**, I'm so proud of him.

1191- Une crainte – *A fear*

Je n'ai qu'une seule **crainte** : me retrouver seule.
I only have one **fear**: ending up alone.

1192- Commettre – *To commit*

Ce soir, il va **commettre** un crime.
Tonight, he will **commit** a crime.

1193- Précisément – *Precisely*

C'est **précisément** ce que je voulais dire.
This is **precisely** what I meant to say.

1194- Un soutien – *Support*

J'ai vraiment besoin de ton **soutien** pendant ce moment difficile.
I really need your **support** during this difficult time.

1195- Facilement – *Easily*

Grâce à ses roulettes, cette chaise peut être déplacée **facilement**.
Thanks to its casters, this chair can be moved **easily**.

1196- Une urgence – *An emergency*

Appelle-moi immédiatement, c'est **une urgence**.
Call me immediately, it's **an emergency**.

1197- Une clé – *A key*

J'ai encore oublié mes **clés** sur la table.
I forgot my **keys** on the table again.

1198- Jeter – *To throw away*

Je suis très attachée à cette photo, ne la **jette** pas!
I'm very attached to this photo, don't **throw** it **away**!

1199- Religieux|Religieuse – *Religious*

Son appartement est rempli de symboles **religieux**.
Her apartment is filled with **religious** symbols.

1200- Une analyse – *An analysis*

Je vais maintenant procéder à **l'analyse** des données.
I will now proceed with **the analysis** of the data.

1201- Disponible – *Available*

Ce siège est-il **disponible**?
Is this seat **available**?

1202- Un regard – *A look*

Elle m'a lancé **un regard** à la fois perçant et effrayant.
She gave me **a look** both piercing and frightening.

1203- Prévenir – *To prevent/To warn*

Afin de **prévenir** une catastrophe, j'ai préféré te **prévenir**.
To **prevent** a catastrophy, I preferred **to warn** you.

1204- Enlever – *To remove*

Veuillez **enlever** vos souliers avant d'entrer.
Please **remove** your shoes before coming in.

1205- Analyser – *To analyse*

Laisse-moi le temps d'**analyser** la situation.
Give me some time **to analyse** the situation.

1206- Un mariage – *A wedding/Marriage*

N'oublis pas : c'est **le mariage** de ton cousin ce weekend.
Don't forget: it's your cousin's **wedding** this weekend.

1207- Une couleur – *A color*

Je préfèrerais **une couleur** neutre pour la salle de bain.
I would prefer a neutral **color** for the bathroom.

1208- Témoigner – *To testify*

Il va **témoigner** devant le juge à neuf heures.
He will **testify** in front of the judge at nine o'clock.

1209- Sauver – *To save*

Je te dois tout, tu m'as **sauvé** la vie.
I owe you everything, you **saved** my life.

1210- Bientôt – *Soon*

J'espère qu'on se reverra **bientôt**.
I hope we'll see each other again **soon**.

1211- Une conclusion – *A conclusion*

Quand j'écris une dissertation, je commence toujours par **la conclusion**.
When I write an essay, I always begin with **the conclusion**.

1212- Bleu|Bleue – *Blue*

Cet oiseau **bleu** vient du Brézil.
This **blue** bird is from Brazil.

1213- Dehors – *Outside*

Le chien a envie d'aller **dehors**.
The dog wants to go **outside**.

1214- Remercier – *To thank*

Je vous **remercie** pour l'invitation.
I **thank** you for the invitation.

1215- Actif|Active – *Active*

Mon père devrait avoir un mode de vie plus **actif**.

My father should have a more **active** lifestyle.

1216- Réclamer – *To claim*

Vous devez vous rendre au secrétariat pour **réclamer** un objet perdu.
You need to get to the secretary's office **to claim** a lost object.

1217- Parlementaire – *Parliamentary*

Nous avons besoin d'une réforme **parlementaire**.
We need a **parliamentary** reform.

1218- Un climat – *Climate*

L'Australie a **un climat** tres chaud.
Australia has a very hot **climate**.

1219- Récemment – *Recently*

Elle est toujours en colère **récemment**, je ne sais pas quoi faire.
She's always angry **recently**, I don't know what to do.

1220- Un fil – *A thread*

Le fil rouge sur un fond blanc crée un joli contraste.
The red **thread** on a white background creates a nice contrast.

1221- Collectif|Collective – *Collective*

Cet événement s'inscrit dans la mémoire **collective** des citoyens.
This event falls within the **collective** memory of the citizens.

1222- Excellent|Excellente – *Excellent*

Quelle **excellente** façon de débuter la semaine!
What an **excellent** way to start the week!

1223- Un moral – *A morale*

J'ignore comment leur remonter **le moral**.
I don't know how to boost their **morale**.

1224- Une habitude – *A habit*

Arrête de te ronger les ongles, c'est une mauvaise **habitude**.
Stop biting your nails, it's a bad **habit**.

1225- Un code – *A code*

Il refuse de me donner **le code** d'accès pour le coffre-fort.
He refuses to give me the access **code** for the safe.

1226- Puissant|Puissante – *Powerful*

L'amour est le sentiment le plus **puissant**.
Love is the most **powerful** feeling.

1227- Recueillir – *To collect*

Je dois **recueillir** plus d'informations avant de pouvoir donner mon opinion.
I need **to collect** more information before I can give my opinion.

1228- Fabriquer – *To manufacture/To make*

Ce produit est **fabriqué** en Chine.
This product is **manufactured** in China.

1229- Représentant|Représentante – *Representative*

J'ai une rencontre avec **la représentante** de cet organisme.
I have a meeting with **the representative** of this organism.

1230- Un accident – *An accident*

Après **l'accident**, elle n'était plus la même.
After **the accident**, she was not the same.

1231- Extraordinaire – *Extraordinary*

Ce spectacle de magie était **extraordinaire**.
This magic show was **extraordinary**.

1232- Dimanche – *Sunday*

Beaucoup vont encore à l'église tous les **dimanches**.
Many still go to church every **Sunday**.

1233- Vérifier – *To check*

Laisse-moi **vérifier**, je reviens dans une minute.
Let me **check**, I'll be back in a minute.

1234- Une envie – *A desire*

J'ai **une envie** inexplicable de manger des cornichons.
I have an unexplainable **desire** to eat pickles.

1235- Enregistrer – *To record*

Elle ne le sait pas, mais j'ai **enregistré** notre conversation.
She doesn't know it, but I **recorded** our conversation.

1236- Rare – *Rare*

Cette espèce d'oiseau est très **rare**.
This bird species is very **rare**.

1237- Un parc – *A park*

Le parc sera fermé ce mercredi.
The park will be closed this Wednesday.

1238- Un impôt – *A tax*

Mon copain fait son propre rapport d'**impôt**.
My boyfriend does his own **tax** return.

1239- Sud – *South*

Ce magasin est un peu plus au **sud**.
This shop is a little more to the **South**.

1240- Efficace – *Efficient*

C'est une façon très **efficace** de soulager la douleur.
It's a very **efficient** way to relieve pain.

1241- Intéressant|Intéressante – *Interesting*

La leçon d'aujourd'hui était très **intéressante**.
Today's lesson was very **interesting**.

1242- Une île – *An island*

Il est tellement riche qu'il a acheté sa propre **île** privée.
He's so rich that he bought his own private **island**.

1243- Une cité – *A city*

La cité d'Atlantide est une légende.
The city of Atlantis is a legend.

1244- Moderne – *Modern*

Son appartement a un style très **moderne**.
Her apartment has a very **modern** style.

1245- Voter – *To vote*

Pour qui vas-tu **voter**?
Who will you **vote** for?

1246- Un traité – *A treaty*

Je n'arrive pas à croire qu'il ait refusé de signer **le traité** de paix.
I can't believe he refused to sign the peace **treaty**.

1247- Une libération – *A liberation*

La libération des otages a eu lieu tôt ce matin.
The liberation of the hostages happened early this morning.

1248- Nourrir – *To feed*

J'ai besoin de cet emploi, j'ai trois bouches à **nourrir**.
I need this job, I have three mouths **to feed**.

1249- Sérieusement – *Seriously*

Tu ne croyais pas **sérieusement** que ce serait aussi simple.
You didn't **seriously** think it would be that easy.

1250- Une carrière – *A career*

Sa **carrière** passera toujours en premier.
His **career** will always come first.

1251- Immédiat|Immédiate – *Immediate*

J'ai besoin de votre réponse **immédiate**, commandant.
I need your **immediate** response, commander.

1252- Exceptionnel|Exceptionnelle – *Exceptional*

Tu as un talent **exceptionnel**, j'espère que tu le sais.
You have an **exceptional** talent, I hope you know it.

1253- Rechercher – *To look for*

Je **recherche** la première édition de ce livre depuis vingt ans.
I have been **looking for** the first edition of this book for twenty years.

1254- Palestinien|Palestinienne – *Palestinian*

Nous entendons parler du conflit israélo-**palestinien** tous les jours.

We hear about the Israeli-**Palestinian** conflict every day.

1255- Un bras – *An arm*

Elle était tellement en colère qu'elle a menacé de lui casser **le bras**.
She was so angry that she threatened to break his **arm**.

1256- Producteur|Productrice – *Producer*

Mon ami Théodore est **producteur** de musique en Californie.
My friend Théodore is a music **producer** in California.

1257- Garantir – *To guarantee*

Cette entreprise fait tout pour **garantir** la satisfaction des clients.
This business does everything **to guarantee** client satisfaction.

1258- Un geste – *A gesture*

Tous les participants ont apprécié son **geste**.
All the participants appreciated his **gesture**.

1259- Un roman – *A novel*

Je rêve d'écrire **un roman** un jour.
I dream of writing **a novel** one day.

1260- Une augmentation – *An increase*

Je constate **une augmentation** de votre glycémie.
I notice **an increase** in your blood glucose.

1261- Le lendemain – *The next day*

Elle a été malade, mais elle se sentait mieux **le lendemain**.
She was sick, but she felt better **the next day**.

1262- Policier|Policière – *Policeman|Policewoman*

Le policier lui a donné une contravention pour excès de vitesse.
The policeman gave him a speeding ticket.

1263- Une échelle – *A ladder*

J'ai peur qu'il tombe de **l'échelle**, elle n'a pas l'air stable.
I'm afraid he's going to fall off **the ladder**, it doesn't look steady.

1264- Supplémentaire – *Additional*

Nous pouvons vous l'expédier directement pour un frais
supplémentaire.
We can ship it to you directly for an **additional** fee.

1265- Pratiquer – *To practice*

Je n'ai pas eu le temps de **pratiquer** mes gammes cette semaine.
I didn't have time **to practice** my scales this week.

1266- Une pensée – *A thought*

Ne me remercie pas, ce n'était qu'une petite **pensée**.
Don't thank me, it was only a small **thought**.

1267- Un facteur – *A factor*

La coopération est **le facteur** clé de la réussite.
Cooperation is the key **factor** to success.

1268- Néanmoins – *Nevertheless*

Il était **néanmoins** très fatigué.
He was very tired, **nevertheless**.

1269- Bénéficier – *To benefit*

Cette entreprise **bénéficierait** beaucoup d'une relocalisation.
This business **would benefit** a lot from a relocation.

1270- Vingt – *Twenty*

Je suis prise à l'aéroport depuis **vingt** heures.
I have been stuck at the airport for **twenty** hours.

1271- Revoir – *To see again*

Quand allons-nous nous **revoir**?
When will we **see** each other **again**?

1272- Extrême – *Extreme*

Je ne peux pas prendre ma voiture dans ces conditions **extrêmes**.
I can't take my car in these **extreme** conditions.

1273- Un défaut – *A fault*

Je l'aimerai toujours malgré ses **défauts**.
I will always love him despite his **faults**.

1274- Précieux|Précieuse – *Precious*

Cette bague est mon bien le plus **précieux**.
This ring is my most **precious** belonging.

1275- Un retard – *A delay*

Le train aura **un retard** de cinq minutes.
The train will have a five-minute **delay**.

1276- Une démocratie – *A democracy*

Ce pays n'a jamais connu **la démocratie**.
This country has never known **democracy**.

1277- Renforcer – *To reinforce/To strenghten*

La structure en acier **renforce** cette échelle.
The steel structure **reinforces** this ladder.

1278- Le silence – *Silence*

J'ai besoin de **silence** pour me concentrer.
I need **silence** to concentrate.

1279- Une perspective – *A perspective*

Ceci te permettra de voir les choses sous une **perspective** différente.
This will allow you to see things under a different **perspective**.

1280- Qualifier – *To qualify*

Je ne peux pas **qualifier** ce commentaire comme « utile ».
I can't **qualify** this comment as "useful".

1281- Absolu|Absolue – *Absolute*

En hiver, la température est souvent sous le zéro **absolu**.
In the winter, the temperature is often under **absolute** zero.

1282- Dégager – *To clear*

Essayez de **dégager** un chemin pour les piétons.
Try **to clear** a path for the pedestrians.

1283- Une stratégie – *A strategy*

J'ai gagné, car j'avais une meilleure **stratégie** que mon adversaire.
I won, because I had a better **strategy** than my opponent.

1284- Un bateau – *A boat*

Marcel vient de s'acheter **un bateau**; il n'a jamais été aussi heureux.
Marcel just bought **a boat**; he's never been this happy.

1285- Une troupe – *A troupe*

J'ai auditionné pour faire partie de cette **troupe** de théâtre.
I auditioned to be a part of this theater **troupe**.

1286- Une course – *A race*

Je m'entraîne depuis des mois pour gagner cette **course**.

I have been training for months to win this **race**.

1287- Un exercice – *An exercise*

Mon entraîneur m'a recommendé d'essayer un nouveau **exercice**.
My trainer has recommended I tried a new **exercise**.

1288- Fondamental|Fondamentale – *Fundamental*

Le respect est une chose **fondamentale**.
Respect is a **fundamental** thing.

1289- Un visage – *A face*

Qui est-ce? Je ne reconnais pas son **visage**.
Who is this? I don't recognize his **face**.

1290- Le printemps – *Spring*

J'ai déjà hâte au **printemps** prochain.
I already can't wait for next **Spring**.

1291- Une machine – *A machine*

Cette **machine** sert à trier les légumes.
This **machine** is used to sort vegetables.

1292- Un village – *A village*

Mes grand-parents habitent dans un petit **village**.
My grandparents live in a small **village**.

1293- Britannique – *British*

Cette entreprise contribue à l'économie **britannique**.
This business contributes to the **British** economy.

1294- Surveiller – *To watch*

Je ne peux pas venir, je dois **surveiller** mon petit frère.

I can't come, I need **to watch** my little brother.

1295- Une édition – *An edition*

Ils ont sorti **une édition** limitée de cet album.
They released a limited **edition** of this album.

1296- La droite – *The right*

Déplace la table un peu plus vers **la droite**.
Move the table a little more to **the right**.

1297- Un organisme – *An organism*

Je fais du bénévolat pour **un organisme** humanitaire.
I volunteer for a humanitarian **organism**.

1298- Une leçon – *A lesson*

Cet accident t'a appris une bonne **leçon**.
This accident taught you a valuable **lesson**.

1299- Décevoir – *To disappoint*

Pardonnez-moi, je ne voulais pas vous **décevoir**.
Forgive me, I did not mean **to disappoint** you.

1300- Une bataille – *A battle*

C'est toujours dur de perdre **une bataille**.
It's always hard to lose **a battle**.

1301- Un port – *A harbour*

Le bateau arrivera bientôt au **port**.
The boat will soon arrive to the **harbor**.

1302- Une naissance – *A birth*

Elle a toujours été curieuse, même depuis sa **naissance**.

She has always been curious, even since her **birth**.

1303- Majeur|Majeure – *Major*

Tu as commis une faute **majeure**.
You have committed a **major** fault.

1304- Accomplir – *To accomplish*

Pense à ce que nous pourrions **accomplir** ensemble.
Think of what we could **accomplish** together.

1305- Un hôpital – *A hospital*

J'irai visiter ma mère à **l'hôpital** demain matin.
I'll go visit my mother at **the hospital** tomorrow morning.

1306- Un circuit – *A circuit*

Le courrant ne passe pas si **le circuit** est fermé.
The current doesn't flow if **the circuit** is closed.

1307- Terrible – *Terrible*

J'ai de **terribles** nouvelles à t'annoncer.
I have **terrible** news to tell you.

1308- Un degré – *A degree*

L'inclinaison doit être à un plus haut **degré**.
The inclination has to be at a higher **degree**.

1309- Une exigence – *A demand*

Mon patron a toujours de nouvelles **exigences**.
My boss always has new **demands**.

1310- Un rêve – *A dream*

Il vit son **rêve** de voyager à travers le monde.

He is living his **dream** to travel around the world.

1311- Le froid – *The cold*

Ce que j'aime le moins du Canada, c'est **le froid**.
What I like the least about Canada is **the cold**.

1312- Opérer – *To operate*

La blessure est trop sérieuse, nous allons devoir **opérer**.
The injury is too serious, we will need **to operate**.

1313- Entièrement – *Entirely*

Ce n'est pas **entièrement** de ma faute.
It's not **entirely** my fault.

1314- Un chapitre – *A chapter*

Je viens de commencer ce livre, je suis encore au premier **chapitre**.
I just started this book, I'm still on the first **chapter**.

1315- Quotidien|Quotidienne – *Daily*

Sa routine **quotidienne** semble très ennuyante.
Her **daily** routine seems very boring.

1316- Clairement – *Clearly*

Je te vois beaucoup plus **clairement** avec mes nouvelles lunettes.
I see you a lot more **clearly** with my new glasses.

1317- Inspirer – *To inspire*

Il a choisi la politique pour **inspirer** les gens.
He chose politics **to inspire** people.

1318- Léger|Légère – *Light(weight)*

Cette crème a un goût très **léger**.

This cream has a very **light** taste.

1319- Permanent|Permanente – *Permanent*

Ne t'inquiète pas, ce tatouage n'est que semi-**permanent**.
Don't worry, this tattoo is only semi-**permanent**.

1320- Un|Une juge – *A judge*

Le juge prendra la décision finale.
The judge will take the final decision.

1321- Un|Une après-midi – *An afternoon*

Quel bel **après-midi**! Allons dehors.
What a nice **afternoon**! Let's go outside.

1322- Joindre – *To join*

Nous devons commencer par **joindre** les deux extrémités.
We need to start by **joining** the two ends.

1323- Juillet – *July*

Je vais à Toronto en **juillet**.
I'm going to Toronto in **July**.

1324- Ordinaire – *Ordinary*

Cette expérience était complètement hors de l'**ordinaire**.
This experience was completely out of the **ordinary**.

1325- Candidat|Candidate – *Candidate*

Cette **candidate** a beaucoup d'expérience dans le domaine.
This **candidate** has a lot of experience in the field.

1326- Rapprocher – *To bring closer*

Ce voyage nous a définitivement **rapprochés**.

This trip definitely **brought** us **closer** together.

1327- Une résistance – *A resistance*

Il y a trop de **résistance** dans le circuit électrique.
There is too much **resistance** in the electrical circuit.

1328- Russe – *Russian*

Il a un accent **russe** très charmant.
He has a very charming **Russian** accent.

1329- Justement – *Precisely*

C'est **justement** ce que j'essayais de faire.
That's **precisely** what I was trying to do.

1330- Habitant|Habitante – *Inhabitant*

Il y a seulement trois cents **habitants** dans ce village.
There are only three hundred **inhabitants** in this village.

1331- Une formule – *A formula*

Je ne sais pas comment utiliser cette **formule** mathématique.
I don't know how to use this mathematical **formula**.

1332- Un mur – *A wall*

Elle a décidé de peindre les **murs** en rose.
She decided to paint the **walls** pink.

1333- Un tribunal – *A tribunal*

Charles était très nerveux devant **le tribunal**.
Charles was very nervous in front of **the tribunal**.

1334- Fier|Fière – *Proud*

Tu as travaillé très fort, je suis **fière** de toi.

You worked very hard, I'm **proud** of you.

1335- Manger – *To eat*

Il est quatre heures et je n'ai pas encore **mangé**.
It's four o'clock and I haven't **eaten** yet.

1336- Soulever – *To lift up*

Je me suis fait mal en dos en **soulevant** cette boîte.
I hurt my back while **lifting** this box **up**.

1337- Évidemment – *Obviously/Evidently*

Évidemment, c'était beaucoup plus difficile que ce que je croyais au départ.
Obviously, it was a lot harder than I thought at first.

1338- Travailleur|Travailleuse – *Worker*

Ces **travailleurs** ont une bonne convention collective.
These **workers** have a good collective agreement.

1339- Une résolution – *A resolution*

Je n'ai respecté aucune de mes **résolutions** cette année.
I've respected none of my **resolutions** this year.

1340- Un|Une journaliste – *A journalist*

Votre entrevue avec **la journaliste** est à seize heures.
Your interview with **the journalist** is at four PM.

1341- Une marque – *A brand/A mark*

Cette **marque** de vêtements a laissé sa **marque** sur l'industrie.
This clothing **brand** has left its **mark** on the industry.

1342- Une utilisation – *A use*

La garantie ne protège pas contre **une utilisation** inappropriée du produit.
The warranty doesn't protect against improper **use** of the product.

1343- Une offre – *An offer*

Merci pour votre **offre**, je vais y penser.
Thank you for your **offer**, I'll think about it.

1344- Habituel|Habituelle – *Usual*

Elle portait ses bottes noires **habituelles**.
She was wearing her **usual** black boots.

1345- Survivre – *To survive*

Je ne vais pas **survivre** une semaine sans toi.
I won't **survive** one week without you.

1346- Populaire – *Popular*

Cette chanson est très **populaire**, la connais-tu?
This song is very **popular**, do you know it?

1347- Dirigeant|Dirigeante – *A leader*

Nous avons confiance en notre **dirigeant**.
We have faith in our **leader**.

1348- Une participation – *A participation*

Pour ce projet, votre **participation** est requise.
For this project, your **participation** is required.

1349- Une évolution – *An evolution*

Le développement de cette caractéristique est **une évolution** naturelle.

The development of this caracteristic is a natural **evolution**.

1350- Totalement – *Totally*

Je suis **totalement** amoureux de toi.
I'm **totally** in love with you.

1351- Gérer – *To manage*

Je trouve difficile de **gérer** mon temps.
I find it difficult **to manage** my time.

1352- Une constitution – *A constitution*

Cette nouvelle **constitution** a récemment été adoptée.
This new **constitution** was recently adopted.

1353- Informer – *To inform*

Je suis ici pour vous **informer** des plus récents développements.
I'm here **to inform** you of the latest developments.

1354- Fou|Folle – *Crazy*

Ne l'écoute pas, elle est complètement **folle**.
Don't listen to her, she's completely **crazy**.

1355- Attacher – *To tie*

Mon petit frère vient d'apprendre comment **attacher** ses lacets.
My little brother just learned how **to tie** his shoelaces.

1356- Renouveler – *To renew*

Cliquez ici pour **renouveler** votre abonnement.
Click here **to renew** your subscription.

1357- S'assoir – *To sit*

Viens, nous allons **nous assoir** sur ce banc.

Come, we're going **to sit** on this bench.

1358- Samedi – *Saturday*

Samedi, c'est le meilleur jour de la semaine.
Saturday is the best day of the week.

1359- Un transfert – *A transfer*

J'ai besoin de l'argent maintenant, peux-tu me faire **un transfert**?
I need the money now, can you make me **a transfer**?

1360- Renoncer – *To renounce*

Elle a **renoncé** à sa citoyenneté pour aller vivre aux États-Unis.
She **renounced** her citizenship to go live in the United States.

1361- Un roi – *A king*

Stéphane est **le roi** de la danse contemporaine.
Stéphane is **the king** of contemporary dance.

1362- Un téléphone – *A telephone*

Il a encore perdu son **téléphone**.
He lost his **telephone** again.

1363- La foi – *Faith*

Nous avons tous beaucoup de **foi** en ce projet.
We all have a lot of **faith** in this project.

1364- Un motif – *A pattern*

Ce coussin a **un motif** fleuri de couleur rose.
This cushion has a floral **pattern** in a pink color.

1365- Plaindre – *To feel sorry for*

Elle travaille trop, je la **plains**.

She works too much, I **feel sorry for** her.

1366- Une tradition – *A tradition*

Ce banquet annuel est **une tradition** dans ma famille.
This annual banquet is **a tradition** in my family.

1367- Net|Nette – *Clear*

Je comprends, c'est **net** et précis.
I understand, it's **clear** and precise.

1368- Une victoire – *A victory*

Une autre **victoire** pour notre équipe!
Another **victory** for our team!

1369- Un arrêt – *A stop*

Je t'attends à **l'arrêt** d'autobus.
I'm waiting for you at the bus **stop**.

1370- Un concours – *A contest*

Calme-toi, ce n'est pas **un concours**.
Calm down, this isn't **a contest**.

1371- Vis-à-vis – *Face to face*

Nous nous assoyons toujours **vis-à-vis**.
We always sit **face to face**.

1372- Un institut – *An institute*

Elle étudie dans **un institut** réputé.
She studies in a renowned **institute**.

1373- Visiter – *To visit*

Je viendrai te **visiter** cet été.

I will come **visit** you this summer.

1374- Elle-même – *Herself*

Remercie Sandra, elle a tout préparé **elle-même**.
Thank Sandra, she prepared everything **herself**.

1375- Démocratique – *Democratic*

Il a été élu de manière **démocratique**.
He was elected in a **democratic** manner.

1376- Une tentative – *An attempt*

C'est sa deuxième **tentative** de suicide cette année, elle a besoin
d'aide.
It's her second suicide **attempt** this year, she needs help.

1377- Largement – *Widely*

Ce programme est **largement** reconnu au Canada.
This program is **widely** renowned in Canada.

1378- Aboutir – *To end up*

Nous avons pris la mauvaise sortie et avons **abouti** dans une ville
inconnue.
We took the wrong exit and **ended up** in an unknown city.

1379- Désirer – *To desire*

C'est ce que je **désire** plus que tout.
This is what I **desire** most of all.

1380- Une côte – *A coast*

Cette espèce vit de l'autre côté de **la côte**.
This species lives on the other side of **the coast**.

1381- Une génération – *A generation*

J'ai peur que la prochaine **génération** manque de ressources.
I fear that the next **generation** will lack resources.

1382- Le vent – *The wind*

Le vent est très fort aujourd'hui, soit prudent.
The wind is very strong today, be careful.

1383- La technologie – *Technology*

André est fasciné par les nouvelles **technologies**.
André is fascinated by new **technologies**.

1384- Échouer – To fail

J'ai vraiment peur d'**échouer** mon examen.
I'm really afraid I'll **fail** my exam.

1385- En dépit – *In spite*

La fête aura lieu **en dépit** des récents événements.
The party will be held **in spite** of the recent events.

1386- Un équilibre – *A balance*

Tu dois trouver **un équilibre** entre la famille et le travail.
You must find **a balance** between family and friends.

1387- Inquiet|Inquiète – *Worried*

Où étais-tu? J'étais tellement **inquiète**.
Where were you? I was so **worried**.

1388- Un obstacle – *An obstacle*

Elle n'a pas pu éviter **l'obstacle** sur la route.
She couldn't avoid **the obstacle** on the road.

1389- Une réflexion – *A reflection*

Cette proposition demande **une réflexion**.
This proposition asks for **a reflection**.

1390- S'inquiéter – *To worry*

Je **m'inquiète** tout le temps pour rien.
I always **worry** for nothing.

1391- Affecter – *To affect*

Sa décision a beaucoup **affecté** notre relation.
His decision has **affected** our relationship a lot.

1392- Une revanche – *A revenge*

J'ai perdu les trois dernières parties, je veux ma **revanche**!
I lost the three last games, I want my **revenge**!

1393- Ressembler – *To resemble*

Ce nuage **ressemble** à un chat.
This cloud **resembles** a cat.

1394- Une station – *A station*

Je l'ai rencontré à **la station** d'essence.
I met him at the gas **station**.

1395- Uniquement – *Only*

Il n'est pas **uniquement** pompier, il est aussi écrivain.
He is not **only** a fireman, he is also a writer.

1396- Supporter – *To support*

Je serai toujours là pour te **supporter**.
I will always be there **to support** you.

1397- Une catégorie – *A category*

Vous devez choisir trois éléments dans cette **catégorie**.
You need to choose three elements in this **category**.

1398- Une mine – *A mine*

Victor est ingénieur, il travaille dans **une mine**.
Victor is an engineer, he works in **a mine**.

1399- Législatif|Législative – *Legislative*

Ils nous ont assuré que le processus **législatif** serait respecté.
They've assured us that the **legislative** process would be respected.

1400- Le|La propriétaire – *The owner*

Le propriétaire de l'immeuble est responsable de l'entretien.
The owner of the building is responsible for the maintenance.

1401- Favoriser – *To favor*

Cette décision a été prise pour **favoriser** l'équipe.
This decision was taken **to favor** the team.

1402- Privé|Privée – *Private*

Allez-vous-en, ceci est une propriété **privée**!
Go away, this is **private** property!

1403- Un avion – *A plane*

Je suis toujours malade dans **l'avion**.
I'm always sick on the **plane**.

1404- Minimum – *Minimum*

Faites le **minimum** de bruit possible, j'essaie de dormir.
Make as **minimum** noise as possible, I'm trying to sleep.

1405- Criminel|Criminelle – *Criminal*

Ils ont finalement arrêté ce **criminel** dangereux.
They have finally arrested this dangerous **criminal**.

1406- Une photo – *A photo*

Je garde cette **photo** de lui dans mon portefeuille.
I keep this **photo** of him in my wallet.

1407- Précéder – *To precede*

Le juge a complètement ignoré les événements qui avaient
précédé.
The judge completely ignored the events that had **preceded**.

1408- Solide – *Solid*

Ses arguments ne sont pas très **solides**.
His arguments aren't very **solid**.

1409- Une priorité – *A priority*

Les piétons ont **la priorité**.
The pedestrians have **the priority**.

1410- Un navire – *A ship*

J'aurais aimé voir les anciens **navires** français.
I would have loved to see the ancient French **ships**.

1411- Une centaine – *A hundred*

Il devait y avoir **une centaine** de personnes à la fête hier soir!
There must have been **a hundred** people at the party last night!

1412- Une explication – *An explanation*

Pourquoi as-tu fait ça? J'attends **une explication**.
Why did you do that? I'm waiting for **an explanation**.

1413- Transmettre – *To transmit*

Merci, mais j'ai déjà **transmis** une requête à
l'administrateur.Thank you, but I've already **transmitted** a
request to the administrator.

1414- Un appareil – *A device*

L'appreil doit être placé à six pieds du mur.
The device must be placed six feet away from the wall.

1415- Correspondre – *To correspond*

Le sujet de votre projet doit **correspondre** à ce dont nous avons
parlé hier.
The subject of your project must **correspond** to what we talked
about yesterday.

1416- Associer – *To associate*

Il est **associé** à l'une des plus grandes entreprises d'Europe.
He's **associated** to one of the largest companies in Europe.

1417- Un trait – *A trait*

Elle est très drôle, je trouve **ce trait** charmant.
She's very funny, I find **this trait** charming.

1418- Une référence – *A reference*

Ce film faisait **une référence** aux Jeux Olympiques.
This movie made **a reference** to the Olympic Games.

1419- Le bois – *The wood*

Cette table en **bois** de pin est magnifique.
This pine **wood** table is magnificent.

1420- Une publication – *A publication*

Il a été forcé de supprimer sa **publication** blessante.
He was forced to delete his offensive **publication**.

1421- Un symbole – *A symbol*

Cette bague est **un symbole** de notre amour.
This ring is **a symbol** of our love.

1422- La consommation – *The consumption*

La consommation de breuvages alcoolisés est interdite sur la terrasse.
The consumption of alcoholic beverages is forbidden on the terrace.

1423- Idéal|Idéale – *Ideal*

Cet endroit est **idéal** pour nos vacances d'été.
This place is **ideal** for our summer vacation.

1424- Le chômage – *Unemployment*

Le taux de **chômage** a encore augmenté cette année.
The **unemployment** rate has increased again this year.

1425- Le courage – *The courage*

Je n'ai pas **le courage** de lui parler.
I don't have **the courage** to talk to her.

1426- Identifier – *To identify*

Pouvez-vous **identifier** votre agresseur parmi ces quatre individus?
Can you **identify** your assailant amidst these four individuals?

1427- Un entretien – An interview/*Maintenance*

Eugène a **un entretien** d'embauche pour devenir préposé à **l'entretien**.

Eugène has a job **interview** to become a **maintenance** worker.

1428- Encourager – *To encourage*

Merci de m'**encourager**, c'est très apprécié.

Thank you for **encouraging** me, it's very appreciated.

1429- Un kilomètre – *A kilometer*

Il est parti travailler à des milliers de **kilomètres** de sa ville natale.

He went off to work thousands of **kilometers** away from his hometown.

1430- Dérouler – *To unroll*

Aide-moi à **dérouler** le tapis, nous allons le placer dans ta chambre.

Help me **unroll** the carpet, we're going to place it in your room.

1431- Une identité – *An identity*

L'identité du meurtrier n'a pas encore été découverte.

The murderer's **identity** has not been discovered yet.

1432- La reconnaissance – *Recognition*

Tout son travail lui a apporté beaucoup de **reconnaissance**.

All of her work brought her a lot of **recognition**.

1433- Signaler – *To report*

Elle est allée **signaler** l'incident au garde de sécurité.

She went **to report** the incident to the security guard.

1434- Une division – *A division*

J'ai entendu dire qu'il travaillait pour **une division** du gouvernement.
I heard that he was working for **a division** of the government.

1435- Un contexte – *A context*

Ce mot est plus facile à comprendre en **contexte**.
This word is easier to understand in **context**.

1436- Coupable – *Guilty*

Il est **coupable** d'avoir volé des cigarettes derrière le comptoir.
He is **guilty** of having stolen cigarettes behind the counter.

1437- Favorable – *Favorable*

Nous irons au parc quand la météo sera plus **favorable**.
We will go to the park when the weather is more **favorable**.

1438- Un amendement – *An amendment*

Trois des députés sont en faveur de cet **amendement**.
Three of the deputees are in favor of this **amendment**.

1439- Août – *August*

Il reviendra de voyage le sept **août**.
He will come back from his trip on **August** seventh.

1440- Attribuer – *To attribute*

Tu ne peux pas lui **attribuer** tout le mérite.
You can't **attribute** all the merit to him.

1441- Courir – *To run*

Cours, ou tu manqueras l'autobus!
Run, or you'll miss the bus!

1442- Un examen – *An exam*

Il ne me reste plus qu'**un examen**, puis c'est les vacances.
I only have **one exam** left, then it's the holidays.

1443- Un personnage – *A character*

Sharon est mon **personnage** favori dans cette série télé.
Sharon is my favorite **character** in this TV series.

1444- Une obligation – *An obligation*

Vous devez signer le document, c'est **une obligation**.
You must sign the document, it's **an obligation**.

1445- Inconnu|Inconnue – *Unknown*

Nous nous sommes retrouvés sur un territoire **inconnu**.
We found ourselves in an **unknown** territory.

1446- Échanger – *To exchange*

Je vous appellerai ce soir pour **échanger** quelques mots.
I will call you later **to exchange** a few words.

1447- Un montant – *An amount*

Le montant d'argent nécessaire est trop élevé pour moi.
The necessary **amount** of money is too high for me.

1448- Éliminer – *To eliminate*

Nous travaillons fort pour **éliminer** toutes vos inquiétudes.
We work hard **to eliminate** all of your concerns.

1449- Dénoncer – *To denounce*

Cette injustice doit être **dénoncée**.
This injustice has to be **denounced**.

1450- Un tableau – *A board*

Certaines classes ont encore **un tableau** noir.
Some classrooms still have a black**board**.

1451- Exclure – *To exclude*

Nous ne pouvons pas **exclure** la possibilité qu'il arrive en retard.
We can't **exclude** the possibility that he'll arrive late.

1452- Un meurtre – *A murder*

Le meurtre a été commis pendant la nuit.
The murder was committed during the night.

1453- Un exemplaire – *A copy*

Je vais lui demander de signer mon **exemplaire** de son livre.
I will ask him to sign my **copy** of his book.

1454- Une propriété – *A property*

Cette terre est la **propriété** de ma famille depuis des centaines d'années.
This land has been my family's **property** for hundreds of years.

1455- Final|Finale – *Final*

Je ne suis pas encore prêt à remettre la version **finale**.
I am not ready to hand in the **final** version yet.

1456- Un site – *A site*

Des clôtures nous empêchent d'entrer sur **le site**.
Fences prevent us from entering **the site**.

1457- Une séance – *A session*

On se revoit dans une semaine pour la prochaine **séance**.
I'll see you in one week for the next **session**.

1458- Une ouverture – *An opening*

Il y a **une ouverture** au bas de la cannette.
There is **an opening** at the bottom of the can.

1459- Élire – *To elect*

Nous avons le pouvoir d'**élire** nos représentants.
We have the power **to elect** our representatives.

1460- Une baisse – *A drop*

Les profits ont subi **une baisse** importante cette année.
The profits were subjected to an important **drop** this year.

1461- Une inquiétude – *A concern*

Nous nous occuperons de faire disparaître vos **inquiétudes**.
We will take it upon ourselves to make your **concerns** disappear.

1462- Israélien|Israélienne – *Israeli*

Le représentant **israélien** fera un discours cet après-midi.
The **Israeli** representative will make a speech this afternoon.

1463- Une représentation – *A representation*

Nous irons voir **la représentation** de vingt heures au cinéma.
We will go see the eight PM **representation** at the movie theater.

1464- Une durée – *A duration*

Vous devez respecter cette règle pendant toute **la durée** du contrat.
You must respect this rule during the entire **duration** of the contract.

1465- Un mandat – *A mandate*

Cet engagement fait partie de notre **mandat**.
This commitment is part of our **mandate**.

1466- Quinze – *Fifteen*

Tiens bon, il ne te reste que **quinze** minutes de classe.
Hold on, you only have **fifteen** minutes of class left.

1467- Vide – *Empty*

Comment se fait-il que la bouteille soit déjà **vide**?
How come the bottle is already **empty**?

1468- Un statut – *A status*

J'ignore quel est son **statut** matrimonial.
I don't know what her matrimonial **status** is.

1469- Un essai – *A try*

Devine la nouvelle, tu as droit à trois **essais**!
Guess the news, you're allowed three **tries**!

1470- Pareil|Pareille – *The same*

Ce collier est **pareil** à celui que ma mère m'a acheté.
This necklace is **the same** as the one my mother bought for me.

1471- Italien|Italienne – *Italian*

J'adore ce restaurant **italien**.
I love this **Italian** restaurant.

1472- Suggérer – *To suggest*

Appelle-moi ce soir, j'ai quelque chose à te **suggérer**.
Call me tonight, I have something **to suggest** to you.

1473- Interrompre – *To interrupt*

Ce processus pourrait **interrompre** le transfert des données.
This process could **interrupt** the data transfer.

1474- Au-dessus – *Above*

J'ai placé l'urne sur une tablette **au-dessus** de la cheminée.
I placed the urn on a shelf **above** the fireplace.

1475- Une agence – *An agency*

Je travaille pour **une agence** de recherche.
I work for a research **agency**.

1476- Une usine – *A factory*

Ce produit est fabriqué par nos experts directement dans **l'usine**.
This product is manufactured by our experts directly in **the factory**.

1477- Unir – *To unite*

Nous devons nous **unir** contre cette injustice.
We must **unite** against this injustice.

1478- Sourire – *To smile*

Elle ne **sourit** sur aucune de ses photos.
She doesn't **smile** on any of her photos.

1479- Employé|Employée – *Employee*

Il mérite le titre d'**employé** du mois.
He deserves the title of **employee** of the month.

1480- Un sommet – *A summit*

Nous prendrons une pause une fois arrivés au **sommet**.
We'll take a break once we arrive at the **summit**.

1481- Franchir – *To overcome*

J'ai besoin d'aide pour **franchir** cet obstacle.
I need help to **overcome** this obstacle.

1482- Évident|Évidente – *Obvious*

Malgré son sourire, sa souffrance est **évidente**.
Despite her smile, her suffering is **obvious**.

1483- Un comportement – *A behavior*

Son **comportement** a changé.
His **behavior** has changed.

1484- Une fête – *A party*

Pourquoi n'es-tu pas venu à **la fête** hier soir?
Why didn't you come to **the party** last night?

1485- Un rang – *A rank*

Il peut faire ce qu'il veut, son **rang** social le lui permet.
He can do whatever he wants, his social **rank** allows it.

1486- Écarter – *To keep away*

Écarte cette feuille de papier de la chandelle.
Keep this sheet of paper **away** from the candle.

1487- Une vague – *A wave*

Il s'est fait emporter par **les vagues**.
He was carried away by **the waves**.

1488- Une réduction – *A reduction*

Ce magasin offre **une réduction** de vingt pourcents pour une durée limitée!
This shop offers a twenty-percent **reduction** for a limited time!

1489- Culturel|Culturelle – *Cultural*

Nous devons résoudre ce conflit **culturel**.
We must resolve this **cultural** conflict.

1490- La collaboration – *Collaboration*

Je vous remercie de votre **collaboration**.
I thank you for your **collaboration**.

1491- Le sol – *The floor*

Pas de chien à table, il mangera sur **le sol**!
No dogs at the table, he will eat on **the floor**!

1492- Une taille – *A size*

Cette robe est magnifique, j'espère qu'ils ont ma **taille**.
This dress is beautiful, I hope they have it in my **size**.

1493- Une vertu – *A virtue*

La patience est **une vertu**.
Patience is **a virtue**.

1494- Une distance – *A distance*

La distance qu'il y a entre nous est insupportable.
The distance between us is unbearable.

1495- Un automne – *Autumn*

L'automne est ma saison favorite.
Autumn is my favorite season.

1496- Un arrière – *A back side*

La prise de courant est située à **l'arrière** de l'appareil.
The outlet is situated on **the back side** of the device.

1497- Une vision – *A vision*

Elle a eu **une vision** qui prédisait cet événement.
She had **a vision** that predicted this event.

1498- Investir – *To invest*

Cette année, j'ai choisi d'**investir** dans une nouvelle voiture.
This year, I chose **to invest** in a new car.

1499- Diminuer – *To decrease*

Les revenus de cette entreprise ont **diminué** depuis l'an dernier.
This company's income has **decreased** since last year.

1500- Un contenu – *Contents*

Cette boîte et son **contenu** m'appartiennent.
This box and its **contents** belong to me.

1501- Entourer – *To surround*

La mer **entoure** cette île.
The sea **surrounds** this island.

1502- Juif|Juive – *Jewish*

Sa voiture est tombée en panne dans le quartier **juif**.
His car broke down in the **Jewish** district.

1503- Considérable – *Considerable*

Ceci est une somme **considérable**, laissez-moi y penser.
This is a **considerable** sum, let me think about it.

1504- Une conduite – *A conduct*

Vous devez respecter chaque élément du code de **conduite**.
You must respect every element from the code of **conduct**.

1505- Une convention – *A convention*

La **convention** aura lieu au Palais des Congrès de Montréal.
The **convention** will be held at the Palais des Congrès de Montréal.

1506- Se réfugier – *To take refuge*

Il est allé **se réfugier** au sous-sol pendant l'attaque.
He went **to take refuge** downstairs during the attack.

1507- Prolonger – *To extend*

Son nouveau argument a **prolongé** le débat.
His new argument **extended** the debate.

1508- Verser – *To pour*

Tu as **versé** trop de bière dans mon verre!
You **poured** too much beer in my glass!

1509- Une évidence – *Obvious*

C'est **une évidence** et ça ne peut être contesté.
It is **obvious**, and it cannot be contested.

1510- Essentiellement – *Essentially*

Essentiellement, nous vous demandons de fournir une pièce d'identité.
Essentially, we ask you to provide identification.

1511- Démontrer – *To demonstrate*

Ce rapport **démontre** que la réaction chimique libère de l'énergie.
This report **demonstrates** that the chemical reaction releases energy.

1512- Communiquer – *To communicate*

Notre relation est en péril, parce que nous ne **communiquons** pas assez.

Our relationship is in peril, because we don't **communicate** enough.

1513- Une approche – *An approach*

Il a choisi **une approche** plus humanitaire.
He chose a more humanitarian **approach**.

1514- Un délai – *A delay*

Il y a eu **un délai**, je vais être en retard.
There has been **a delay**, I will be late.

1515- Accroître – *To increase*

Nous espérons **accroître** la qualité de nos produits de manière substantiel.
We hope to substantially **increase** the quality of our products.

1516- Un bruit – *A noise*

J'ai entendu **un bruit**… qui est là?
I heard **a noise**… who's there?

1517- Une humanité – *Humanity*

L'humanité est égoïste, les choses ne changeront jamais.
Humanity is selfish, things will never change.

1518- La radio – *The radio*

J'ai entendu une nouvelle chanson à **la radio**.
I heard a new song on **the radio**.

1519- Moi-même – *Myself*

Si je veux que les choses soient bien faites, je dois les faire **moi-même**.

If I want things to be well done, I need to do them **myself**.

1520- Négatif|Négative – *Negative*

Je ne peux plus tolérer son attitude **négative**.
I can't tolerate her **negative** attitude anymore.

1521- Prudent|Prudente – *Careful*

Sois **prudent** ou tu vas te blesser.
Be **careful** or you'll hurt yourself.

1522- La soirée – *The evening*

J'ai passé une merveilleuse **soirée** avec Bernard.
I spent a wonderful **evening** with Bernard.

1523- Un vol – *A flight/A theft*

Le vol de son portefeuille a dû se produire pendant son **vol** vers Paris.
The theft of her wallet must have happened during her **flight** to Paris.

1524- Marcher – *To walk*

Ce n'est pas loin, on peut y **marcher** jusque là.
It isn't far, we can **walk** there.

1525- Un tiers – *A third*

Elle a déjà complété **un tiers** de son travail.
She has already completed **one third** of her work.

1526- Un mètre – *A meter*

Le prochain arrêt est dans trois cents **mètres**.
The next stop is in three hundred **meters**.

1527- Un syndicat – *A union*

Le syndicat des travailleurs sera bientôt en grève.
The workers' **union** will soon be on strike.

1528- Occidental|Occidentale – *Western*

Patrick préfère la cuisine **occidentale**.
Patrick prefers **Western** cuisine.

1529- Suffisant|Suffisante – *Sufficient*

Cette preuve n'est pas **suffisante** pour l'accuser.
This proof is not **sufficient** to accuse him.

1530- Le ciel – *The sky*

Le ciel est gris, je crois qu'il va pleuvoir.
The sky is grey, I think it's going to rain.

1531- Tromper – *To deceive*

Il a trouvé un moyen de **tromper** son adversaire.
He found a way **to deceive** his opponent.

1532- Modeste – *Modest*

Bienvenue dans notre **modeste** demeure!
Welcome to our **modest** home!

1533- Éloigner – *To move away*

Éloigne ton assiette du rebord de la table.
Move your plate **away** from the edge of the table.

1534- Aborder – *To approach*

Il m'a **abordée** pour une offre d'emploi intéressante.
He **approached** me for an interesting job offer.

1535- Malheureusement – *Unfortunately*

Malheureusement, il n'a pas survécu l'accident.
Unfortunately, he did not survive the accident.

1536- Évaluer – *To evaluate*

Nous devons d'abord **évaluer** la situation.
We first need **to evaluate** the situation.

1537- Extrêmement – *Extremely*

Cette ballerine est **extrêmement** gracieuse.
This ballerina is **extremely** graceful.

1538- Interne – *Internal*

Elle a subi une hémorragie **interne**.
She has suffered an **internal** hemorrhage.

1539- Voire même – *Even*

Elle pourrait quitter le cours, **voire même** quitter le programme.
She could leave the class, **even** leave the program.

1540- Une seconde – *A second*

J'ai jamais pensé à ça, même pas pendant **une seconde**.
I never thought about that, not even for **a second**.

1541- Des messieurs – *Gentlemen*

Veuillez accompagner ces **messieurs** à leur chambre.
Please accompany these **gentlemen** to their room.

1542- Effectivement – *Effectively*

Effectivement, j'avais déjà remarqué.
Effectively, I had already noticed.

1543- Un gaz – *A gas*

L'azote est **un gaz** qui est présent dans l'atmosphère.
Nitrogen is **a gas** that's present in the atmosphere.

1544- Acteur|Actrice – *Actor*

Mon **acteur** favori a remporté un Oscar l'an dernier.
My favorite **actor** won an Oscar last year.

1545- S'adapter – *To adapt*

La nature trouve toujours un moyen de **s'adapter**.
Nature always finds a way **to adapt**.

1546- Un témoignage – *A testimony*

Le juge n'a pas cru son **témoignage**.
The judge did not believe his **testimony**.

1547- Une dépense – *An expense*

Je ne suis pas fier de toi, cette **dépense** était loin d'être nécessaire.
I'm not proud of you, this **expense** was far from necessary.

1548- Un souci – *A worry*

Pas de **soucis**, je m'en occupe.
No **worries**, I'll take care of it.

1549- Expert|Experte – *Expert*

Vincent est **un expert** de la mécanique.
Vincent is **an expert** in mechanical engineering.

1550- Une sœur – *A sister*

Ma **sœur** et moi avons beaucoup en commun.
My **sister** and I have a lot in common.

1551- Relativement – *Relatively*

Il est **relativement** grand pour son âge.
He is **relatively** tall for his age.

1552- Comparer – *To compare*

Tu ne peux pas **comparer** ces deux choses, elles sont trop différentes.
You can't **compare** these two things, they are too different.

1553- Une cour – *A yard*

Nous avons fait un feu dans **la cour**.
We made a fire in **the yard**.

1554- Provenir – *To be from/To come from*

Cette montre **provient** d'Italie.
This watch **comes from** Italy.

1555- Réellement – *Really*

Je ne mens pas, j'ai **réellement** envie de te parler.
I'm not lying, I **really** want to talk to you.

1556- Conscient|Consciente – *Conscious*

Le médecin a dit qu'elle était **consciente**, nous pouvons aller la voir.
The doctor said she was **conscious**, we can go see her.

1557- Céder – *To give up*

Elle avait fait du progrès, mais elle a fini par **céder**.
She had made some progress, but she **gave up** in the end.

1558- Médical|Médicale – *Medical*

Elle ne viendra pas à la rencontre pour des raisons **médicales**.

She will not come to the meeting for **medical** reasons.

1559- Un procès – *A trial*

Avec cet avocat, nous sommes certains de gagner **le procès**.
With this lawyer, we are certain to win **the trial**.

1560- La colère – *Anger*

Tu dois te défaire de toute cette **colère**.
You must get rid of all this **anger**.

1561- Patient|Patiente – *Patient*

Ce **patient** a été très **patient** d'attendre six heures pour les résultats.
This **patient** was very **patient** to wait six hours for the results.

1562- Une notion – *A notion*

Cette **notion** lui est complètement inconnue.
This **notion** is completely unknown to him.

1563- Un siège – *A seat*

Il y a des **sièges** en cuir dans sa voiture.
There are leather **seats** in his car.

1564- Une hausse – *An increase*

Le gouvernement a annoncé **une hausse** du salaire minimum.
The government has announced **an increase** of the minimum wage.

1565- Diviser – *To divide*

Nous devons **diviser** les ressources de manière plus équilibrée.
We must **divide** the resources in a more balanced manner.

1566- Traditionnel|Traditionnelle – *Traditional*

Ceci est une coutume **traditionnelle** en France.
This is a **traditional** custom in France.

1567- Un quart – *A quarter*

Nous auront chacun **un quart** du trésor.
We will each have **one quarter** of the treasure.

1568- Approcher – *To approach*

Le léopard **approche** lentement sa proie.
The leopard slowly **approaches** his prey.

1569- Le trafic – *The traffic*

Je suis prise dans **le trafic** depuis une heure.
I've been stuck in **traffic** for an hour.

1570- Catholique – *Catholic*

Je suis allée à l'école **catholique**.
I went to **Catholic** school.

1571- Un mécanisme – *A mechanism*

Je ne comprends pas comment fonctionne ce **mécanisme**.
I don't understand how this **mechanism** works.

1572- Un|Une adulte – *An adult*

Maryse est **une adulte** responsable, elle saura quoi faire.
Maryse is a responsible **adult**, she'll know what to do.

1573- Reprocher – *To reproach*

Mon père me **reproche** toujours de me lever trop tard.
My father is always **reproaching** me for getting up too late.

1574- Un métier – *A job*

J'ai ce **métier** depuis cinq ans.
I've had this **job** for five years.

1575- Une modification – *A modification*

La **modification** peut seulement être complétée par téléphone.
The **modification** can only be completed by phone.

1576- Peser – *To weigh*

Il **pesait** deux cent trente livres l'an dernier.
He **weighed** two hundred and thirty pounds last year.

1577- Les médias – *The media*

Les **médias** ne doivent pas entendre parler de cette histoire.
The **media** must not hear about that story.

1578- Un foyer – *A home*

Votre **foyer** est si accueillant.
Your **home** is so welcoming.

1579- Une définition – *A definition*

Tu trouveras **la définition** de ce mot dans le dictionnaire.
You will find **the definition** of this word in the dictionary.

1580- Un|Une spécialiste – *A specialist*

Joseph est **un spécialiste** de l'électronique.
Joseph is **a specialist** in electronics.

1581- Un mari – *A husband*

J'attends un appel important de la part de mon **mari**.
I'm waiting for an important call from my **husband**.

1582- Supprimer – *To remove/To delete*

J'ai **supprimé** beaucoup de fichiers de son ordinateur.
I **deleted** a lot of files from his computer.

1583- Guère – *Hardly*

Sans un bon investisseur, notre projet ne pourra **guère** avancer.
Without a good investor, our project will **hardly** move forward.

1584- Douter – *To doubt*

Je **doute** fortement qu'elle veuille me parler.
I highly **doubt** that she wants to talk to me.

1585- Un hiver – *A winter*

L'**hiver** sera froid cette année.
Winter will be cold this year.

1586- Sexuel|Sexuelle – *Sexual*

Pardonne-moi, ce baiser n'avait rien de **sexuel**.
Forgive me, there was nothing **sexual** with this kiss.

1587- Consulter – *To consult*

Elle devrait peut-être **consulter** un psychiatre.
Maybe she should **consult** a psychiatrist.

1588- Un renseignement – *An information*

Je dois appeler la secrétaire pour obtenir **un renseignement**.
I must call the secretary to obtain **an information**.

1589- Âgé|Âgée – *Old*

Ma grand-mère est très **âgée**, mais elle est encore en santé.
My grandmother is very **old**, but she is still healthy.

1590- Ressentir – *To feel*

Il boit pour ne pas **ressentir** la douleur.
He drinks so he won't **feel** the pain.

1591- Le fonctionnement – *The operation*

Voici le manuel de **fonctionnement** de l'appareil.
Here is the **operation** manual of the device.

1592- Un garçon – *A boy*

Ma tante a deux filles et un **garçon**.
My aunt has two girls and **one boy**.

1593- Parfait|Parfaite – *Perfect*

Il est **parfait**, je l'aime de tout mon cœur.
He's **perfect**, I love him with all my heart.

1594- Une prévision – *A forecast*

Quelles sont les **prévisions** météorologiques pour demain?
What's the weather **forecast** for tomorrow?

1595- Quatrième – *Fourth*

Il est arrivé en retard pour la **quatrième** fois ce mois-ci.
He arrived late for the **fourth** time this month.

1596- Une fenêtre – *A window*

Qui a laissé **la fenêtre** ouverte?
Who left **the window** opened?

1597- Incapable – *Incapable*

Ne me dis jamais que je suis **incapable** de quoi que ce soit.
Never tell me I'm **incapable** of anything.

1598- Hésiter – *To hesitate*

Il a **hésité** avant de lancer le ballon.
He **hesitated** before throwing the ball.

1599- Résumer – *To summarize*

Pouvez-vous **résumer** votre projet en cinq minutes?
Can you **summarize** your project in five minutes?

1600- Universel|Universelle – *Universal*

Le langage mathématique est **universel**.
The mathematical language is **universal**.

1601- La jeunesse – *The youth*

Je donnerais n'importe quoi pour ravoir ma **jeunesse**.
I would give anything to have my **youth** back.

1602- Voler – *To steal/To fly*

Il lui a **volé** son pistolet pendant que l'avion **volait** à plus de mille pieds d'altitude.
He **stole** his pistol while the plane was **flying** at an altitude of more than one thousand feet.

1603- Résister – *To resist*

Il est trop charmant, je ne peux pas lui **résister**.
He is too charming, I can't **resist** him.

1604- Profondément – *Profoundly*

Je suis **profondément** désolé de ce que j'ai fait.
I am **profoundly** sorry for what I've done.

1605- Une menace – *A threat*

Ce politicien est **une menace** envers notre société.

This politician is **a threat** to our society.

1606- Inutile – *Useless*

Tous mes efforts ont été **inutiles**.
All my efforts have been **useless**.

1607- Un refus – *A refusal*

Son **refus** de coopérer est frustrant.
His **refusal** to cooperate is frustrating.

1608- Un poisson – *A fish*

Cette animalerie vend des **poissons** exotiques.
This pet shop sells exotic **fish**.

1609- Une révolution – *A revolution*

Ce pays est sur le point de déclencher **une révolution**.
This country is about to start **a revolution**.

1610- Une séparation – *A separation*

Ses parents sont au milieu d'**une séparation**.
His parents are in the middle of **a separation**.

1611- Avouer – *To admit*

Il se sent coupable, mais il ne va jamais l'**avouer**.
He feels guilty, but he will never **admit** it.

1612- Saluer – *To greet/To salute*

Je vous **salue**, mademoiselle.
I **salute** you, miss.

1613- Le fer – *Iron*

L'acier est plus robuste que **le fer**.

Steel is sturdier than **iron**.

1614- Familial|Familiale – *Family*

C'est une tradition **familiale**.
It's a **family** tradition.

1615- Le cinéma – *The cinema*

Nous nous sommes rencontrés au **cinéma**.
We met at **the cinema**.

1616- Prisonnier|Prisonnière – *Prisoner*

Il est **prisonnier** de son propre esprit.
He's a **prisoner** of his own mind.

1617- Armé|Armée – *Armed*

Ils ont arrêté un homme **armé**.
They have arrested an **armed** man.

1618- Un enseignement – *A teaching*

L'**enseignement** est une vocation.
Teaching is a vocation.

1619- Étonnant|Étonnante – *Surprising*

Vous trouverez que les faits sont **étonnants**.
You will find that the facts are **surprising**.

1620- Une dizaine – *Ten*

Il est parti depuis **une dizaine** de jours.
He has been gone for **ten** days.

1621- Sur le dessus – *On (the) top*

Pourais-tu placer mon ordinateur **sur le dessus** de la table s'il-te-

plaît?
Could you please place my computer **on top** of the table?

1622- Un calcul – *A calculation*

On peut obtenir le même résultat avec différents **calculs**.
We can obtain the same result with different **calculations**.

1623- Un|Une fonctionnaire – *A state employee*

Il travaille comme **fonctionnaire** depuis dix ans.
He has worked as a **state employee** for ten years.

1624- Une instruction – *An instruction*

Les **instructions** sont accompagnées de schémas.
The **instructions** are accompanied by diagrams.

1625- Pratiquement – *Practically*

Il n'y a **pratiquement** aucun livre intéressant dans cette
bibliothèque.
There are **practically** no interesting books in this library.

1626- Oser – *To dare*

Elle n'a pas **ôsé** repeindre sa cuisine en jaune.
She didn't **dare** to repaint her kitchen yellow.

1627- Rassembler – *To gather*

Rassemble tous les documents qui concernent ce procès.
Gather every document that has to do with this trial.

1628- Achever – *To complete*

Vous devriez être sur le point d'**achever** votre travail.
You should be on the verge of **completing** your work.

1629- Fiscal|Fiscale – *Fiscal*

Ce drame **fiscal** est partout dans les médias.
This **fiscal** drama is everywhere in the media.

1630- Une démarche – *A process*

Tu as obtenu la bonne réponse, mais ta **démarche** est incomplète.
You got the right answer, but your **process** is incomplete.

1631- Corriger – *To correct*

J'ai soixante-quinze copies à **corriger** pour la semaine prochaine.
I have seventy-five copies **to correct** for next week.

1632- Un volume – *A volume*

Nous avons **un volume** élevé de produits en inventaire.
We have a high **volume** of products in our inventory.

1633- Une réussite – *A success*

Le gala d'hier soir était **une réussite**.
Last night's gala was **a success**.

1634- Un désir – *A desire*

Elle m'a révélé ses **désirs** les plus secrets.
She revealed her most secret **desires** to me.

1635- Une réalisation – *An achievement*

Obtenir un diplôme est une importante **réalisation**.
To obtain a diploma is an important **achievement**.

1636- Une exportation – *An export*

La Floride est reconnue pour l'**exportation** d'oranges.
Florida is renown for **the export** of oranges.

1637- Prier – *To pray*

Je **prie** tous les jours en espérant qu'il ne m'ait pas oubliée.
I **pray** everyday hoping that he hasn't forgotten me.

1638- Trente – *Thirty*

Non merci, le repas de ce midi m'a déjà coûté **trente** dollars.
No thank you, today's lunch already cost me **thirty** dollars.

1639- Une âme – *A soul*

Il a l'air gentil, mais nous savons que son **âme** est impure.
He looks nice, but we know that his **soul** is impure.

1640- Dominer – *To dominate*

Le Brézil a **dominé** cette partie de soccer.
Brazil has **dominated** this soccer game.

1641- Pur|Pure – *Pure*

L'eau de cette source est la plus **pure**.
The water from this spring is the most **pure**.

1642- Un instrument – *An instrument*

Si tu es musicien, alors de quel **instrument** joues-tu?
If you're a musician, then what **instrument** do you play?

1643- Une indépendance – *Independence*

Laisse-le tranquille, il a besoin de son **independence**.
Leave him be, he needs his **independence**.

1644- Un tort – *A wrong*

Tu as **tort**! Jérémie ne ferait jamais une chose pareille.
You're **wrong**! Jérémie would never do such a thing.

1645- La hauteur – *The height*

La hauteur de cette bibliothèque est de sept pieds.
The height of this bookcase is of seven feet.

1646- Critiquer – *To criticize*

Ma mère m'a **critiquée** toute ma vie.
My mother has **criticized** me my entire life.

1647- Une autorisation – *An authorization*

Tu as besoin d'**une autorisation** parentale pour quitter l'école.
You need parental **authorization** to leave school.

1648- Une assurance – *Insurance*

Tous les patients doivent avoir leur propre **assurance** maladie.
Every patient needs to have their own health **insurance**.

1649- Un déficit – *A deficit*

L'entreprise a subi un important **déficit** il y a deux ans.
The company suffered an important **deficit** two years ago.

1650- Évoluer – *To evolve*

Nos sentiments ont **évolué** en quelque chose de différent.
Our feelings have **evolved** into something different.

1651- Une drogue – *A drug*

On oublie souvent que le café est également **une drogue**.
We often forget that coffee is also **a drug**.

1652- Concret|Concrète – *Concrete*

Tes spéculations sont insuffisantes, j'ai besoin d'une idée **concrète**.
Your speculations are insufficient, I need a **concrete** idea.

1653- Une attaque – *An attack*

Des mesures ont été prises pour contrer l'**attaque** terroriste.
Measures have been taken to counter the terrorist **attack**.

1654- Un rythme – *A rhythm/A rate*

Suis **le rythme**! À ce **rythme**, tu n'apprendras jamais à jouer du piano.
Follow **the rhythm**! At this **rate**, you'll never learn how to play the piano.

1655- Approuver – *To approve of*

Mes parents n'**approuvent** pas ma décision.
My parents don't **approve** of my decision.

1656- Douze – *Twelve*

À **douze** ans, mon cousin est déjà un prodige des mathématiques.
At **twelve** years of age, my cousin is already a mathematical prodigy.

1657- Juridique – *Legal*

Certaines procédures **juridiques** n'ont pas été respectées.
Some **legal** procedures have not been respected.

1658- Espagnol|Espagnole – *Spanish*

Ceci est une ancienne tradition **espagnole**.
This is an ancient **Spanish** tradition.

1659- Une saison – *A season*

J'espère qu'il fera chaud cette **saison**.
I hope it will be warm this **season**.

1660- Percevoir – *To perceive*

Nous n'avons pas **perçu** la situation de la même façon.
We haven't **perceived** the situation in the same way.

1661- Une hypothèse – *A hypothesis*

Ce résultat ne nous permettra pas de confirmer **l'hypothèse**.
This result won't allow us to confirm **the hypothesis**.

1662- Relier – *To connect*

Reliez la partie A à la partie B avant de passer à l'étape suivante.
Connect part A to part B before moving on to the next step.

1663- Un financement – *Financing*

Notre projet a grandement besoin de **financement**.
Our project is in great need of **financing**.

1664- Un dos – *A back*

Rester assis toute la journée est mauvais pour **le dos**.
To stay seated all day is bad for the **back**.

1665- Consommateur|Consommatrice – *Consumer/Customer*

Nous essayons satisfaire les besoins des **consommateurs**.
We are trying to satisfy the **customers'** needs.

1666- Une épreuve – *An ordeal*

Ginette a traversé une **épreuve** difficile lorsque son mari est décédé.
Ginette went through a difficult **ordeal** when her husband died.

1667- Volontaire – *Voluntary*

Je suis désolée, ce n'était pas **volontaire**.
I'm sorry, this wasn't **voluntary**.

1668- Négocier – *To negotiate*

Ceci est le prix final, n'essayez pas de **négocier**.
This is the final price, don't try **to negotiate**.

1669- Une finance – *Finance*

Elle étudie **la finance** à l'université.
She studies **finance** at the university.

1670- Rêver – *To dream*

Plusieurs personnes **rêvent** en noir et blanc.
Many people **dream** in black and white.

1671- Indien|Indienne – *Indian*

Essayons ce nouveau restaurant **indien** ce soir.
Let's try this new **Indian** restaurant tonight.

1672- Une quantité – *A quantity*

Cette édition sera disponible dans **une quantité** limitée.
This edition will be available in a limited **quantity**.

1673- Soviétique – *Soviet*

L'Union **soviétique** a signé l'entente.
The **Soviet** Union has signed the agreement.

1674- Persuader – *To persuade*

Il n'a pas pu la **persuader** de venir avec nous.
He couldn't **persuade** her to come with us.

1675- Interpréter – *To interpret*

Il est le seul qui puisse **interpréter** ces symboles.
He is the only one who can **interpret** these symbols.

1676- Annuel|Annuelle – *Annual*

Venez nous voir au magasin pendant notre vente **annuelle**.
Come see us at the shop during out **annual** sale.

1677- Un commentaire – *A comment*

Son **commentaire** m'a fait réfléchir.
His **comment** made me think.

1678- Se marier – *To get married*

J'espère que nous allons **nous marier** un jour.
I hope we'll **get married** one day.

1679- Un spectacle – *A show*

Il y a une autre représentation de ce **spectacle** demain.
There is another representation of this **show** tomorrow.

1680- Un pari – *A bet*

Je t'avais dit que tu allais perdre ton **pari**!
I told you that you were going to lose your **bet**!

1681- Définitif|Définitive – *Definitive*

Est-ce que ceci est la version **définitive** de ton projet?
Is this the **definitive** version of your project?

1682- Ouest – *West*

Un de mes collègues habite plus à l'**ouest**.
One of my colleagues lives further **West**.

1683- Un sexe – *A gender*

Le médecin ne peut pas encore déterminer **le sexe** du bébé.
The doctor can't determine the baby's **gender** yet.

1684- Un recours – *A resort*

Les policiers n'utilisent leur arme à feu qu'en dernier **recours**.
Policemen only use their firearm as a last **resort**.

1685- Un accent – *An accent*

D'où venez-vous? Je ne reconnais pas votre **accent**.
Where do you come from? I don't recognize your **accent**.

1686- Introduire – *To introduce*

Ce reptile ne peut pas être **introduit** dans un habitat différent.
This reptile cannot be **introduced** in a different habitat.

1687- Communiste – *Communist*

L'héritage **communiste** peut encore être observé dans certains pays.
The **Communist** heritage can still be observed in some countries.

1688- Célèbre – *Famous*

Tout le monde rêve de devenir riche et **célèbre**.
Everyone dreams of becoming rich and **famous**.

1689- Une couverture – *A blanket*

Je préfère **la couverture** rouge, où est-elle?
I prefer the red **blanket**, where is it?

1690- Une religion – *A religion*

La religion serait à l'origine de ce conflit.
Religion would be the origin of this conflict.

1691- Un appui – *A support*

Cette chaise possède **un appui** pour la tête en velours.
This chair possesses a velvet **support** for the head.

1692- Un concert – *A concert*

Nous nous sommes rencontrés à **un concert** rock.
We met at a rock **concert**.

1693- Saint|Sainte – *Saint/Holy*

Cette femme est **une sainte**, elle est si généreuse.
This woman is **a saint**, she is so generous.

1694- Conséquent|Conséquente – *Consistent*

Tu ne peux pas dire une chose et en faire une autre; sois
conséquent.
You can't say one thing and do another; be **consistent**.

1695- Un équipement – *An equipment*

Il a oublié son **équipement** dans son camion.
He forgot his **equipment** in his truck.

1696- Descendre – *To go down/To come down*

Pourquoi es-tu sur le toit? **Descends** immédiatement!
Why are you on the roof? **Come down** immediately!

1697- Un théâtre – *A theater*

Ma femme et moi allons au **théâtre** chaque semaine.
My wife and I go to the **theater** every week.

1698- Une marge – *A margin*

J'écrirai mes commentaires dans **la marge**.
I will write my comments in **the margin**.

1699- Un abri – *A shelter*

Nous devons trouver **un abri** pour éviter toute cette pluie.
We must find **shelter** to avoid all this rain.

1700- Une recette – *A recipe*

Il y a une nouvelle **recette** que j'aimerais essayer.
There is a new **recipe** that I would like to try.

1701- Généralement – *Generally*

Ce n'est **généralement** pas le cas, mais nous pouvons faire une exception.
It is **generally** not the case, but we can make an exception.

1702- Une vigueur – *A vigor*

Mon grand-père a **la vigueur** d'un jeune homme.
My grandfather has **the vigor** of a young man.

1703- Un patron – *A boss*

Mon nouveau **patron** veut me rencontrer demain.
My new **boss** wants to meet me tomorrow.

1704- Le soleil – *The sun*

Ne regarde jamais **le soleil** directement.
Never look directly at **the sun**.

1705- Électoral|Électorale – *Electoral*

Maintenant que j'ai dix-huit ans, je serai sur la liste **électorale**.
Now that I'm eighteen years old, I will be on the **electoral** list.

1706- Ennemi|Ennemie – *Enemy*

J'ai appris qu'un ami pouvait facilement devenir un **ennemi**.
I learned that a friend could easily become an **enemy**.

1707- Une bourse – *A scholarship*

J'ai reçu **une bourse** de deux mille dollars pour mes études.
I have received a two-thousand-dollar **scholarship** for my studies.

1708- Une dimension – *A dimension*

Ce film de science-fiction se déroule dans la septième **dimension**.
This science-fiction movie takes place in the seventh **dimension**.

1709- Baser – *To base*

Son argument n'est **basé** sur rien de solide.
His argument is **based** on nothing solid.

1710- Un dialogue – *A dialogue*

Il y a trop d'action et pas assez de **dialogues**.
There is too much action and not enough **dialogues**.

1711- Un thème – *A theme*

Pouvez-vous me dire quel est **le thème** de ce poème?
Can you tell me what this poem's **theme** is?

1712- Circuler – *To circulate*

Circulez, laissez la police faire son travail.
Circulate, let the police do their job.

1713- Un|Une porte-parole – *A spokesperson*

Le porte-parole de cette entreprise a fait une conférence au bureau.
This company's **spokesperson** made a conference at the office.

1714- Une présentation – *A presentation*

Quel sera le sujet de ta **présentation**?
What will the subject of your **presentation** be?

1715- Déployer – *To deploy*

Les soldats ont été **déployés** pendant la nuit.
The soldiers have been **deployed** during the night.

1716- Un outil – *A tool*

Je n'ai pas **l'outil** nécessaire pour accomplir cette tâche.
I don't have the necessary **tool** to accomplish this task.

1717- Une vacance – *A vacation*

Nous sommes actuellement en **vacances** au Mexique.
We are currently on **vacation** in Mexico.

1718- Suffisamment – *Sufficiently/Enough*

J'ai été **suffisamment** surprise pour aujourd'hui; vous en avez fait **suffisamment**.
I have been **sufficiently** surprised for today; you have done **enough**.

1719- Un défi – *A challenge*

C'était un vrai **défi** pour elle, mais elle a eu le courage de le faire.
It was a true **challenge** for her, but she had the courage to do it.

1720- Un front – *A front/A forehead*

Ne te cogne pas **le front** sur **le front** de cette poutre!
Don't bump your **forehead** on **the front** of this beam!

1721- Suspendre – *To suspend*

Marcus a été **suspendu** de l'école parce qu'il s'est battu.
Marcus was **suspended** from school for engaging in a fight.

1722- Une forêt – *A forest*

Suis la carte, je ne veux pas me perdre dans **la forêt**.
Follow the map, I don't want to get lost in **the forest**.

1723- Une montagne – *A mountain*

Nous avons une magnifique vue sur **les montagnes** de notre chambre.

We have a beautiful view of **the mountains** from our room.

1724- Sévère – *Severe*

Sa fracture au crâne est très **sévère**.
His skull fracture is very **severe**.

1725- Apparemment – *Apparently*

Apparemment, il fait toujours très chaud en Arizona.
Apparently, it's always very hot in Arizona.

1726- La présidence – *Presidency*

Elle a laissé **la présidence** lui a monté à la tête; elle est devenue arrogante.
She let **presidency** go to her head; she has become arrogant.

1727- Un magasin – *A shop/A store*

J'ai acheté ce sac à main dans **un magasin** au centre-ville.
I bought this purse in **a store** downtown.

1728- Un|Une commissaire – *A commissioner*

Ce **commissaire** a été choisi par le nouveau premier ministre.
This **commissioner** was chosen by the new Prime Minister.

1729- Calme – *Calm*

Restez **calme**, ce n'était qu'une fausse alerte.
Stay **calm**, this was only a false alarm.

1730- Monétaire – *Monetary*

Mon frère a beaucoup de problèmes **monétaires** en ce moment.
My brothet has a lot of **monetary** issues at the moment.

1731- Un ouvrage – *A work*

Je n'ai pas encore eu le temps de lire le plus récent **ouvrage** de cette écrivaine.
I didn't have time to read this writer's most recent **work** yet.

1732- Une réputation – *A reputation*

Ils ne doivent pas te voir, j'ai **une réputation** à maintenir.
They must not see you, I have **a reputation** to maintain.

1733- Un cabinet – *An office/A practice*

Ma sœur est infirmière, elle travaille dans **un cabinet** médical.
My sister is a nurse, she works in a medical **practice**.

1734- Un écart – *A gap*

L'**écart** ne cesse de grandir entre nous depuis que tu es parti.
The gap between us keeps getting larger since you left.

1735- Un chien – *A dog*

Mon **chien** me suit partout.
My **dog** follows me everywhere.

1736- Écrivain|Écrivaine – *Writer*

J'ai lu tous les ouvrages de cet **écrivain**.
I have read all of this **writer**'s work.

1737- Indispensable – *Indispensable*

Nous vous remercions, votre travail est **indispensable** à notre succès.
We thank you, your work is **indispensable** to our success.

1738- Une conversation – *A conversation*

Elle est tombée amoureuse de lui après une seule **conversation**.
She fell in love with him after only one **conversation**.

1739- Une surface – *A surface*

La **surface** de cette table est faite de marbre.
The **surface** of this table is made of marble.

1740- Féliciter – *To congratulate*

N'oublis pas de **féliciter** ton frère pour son diplôme.
Don't forget **to congratulate** your brother for his diploma.

1741- Sûrement – *Surely*

Éric sera **sûrement** présent à ta fête d'anniversaire.
Éric will **surely** be present at your birthday party.

1742- La surveillance – *Surveillance*

Cet édifice est muni d'un système de **surveillance** moderne.
This building is equipped with a modern **surveillance** system.

1743- Une efficacité – *An efficiency/An effectiveness*

Je ne regrette pas d'avoir engagé Tania, son **efficacité** est remarquable.
I don't regret hiring Tania, her **efficiency** is remarkable.

1744- Un euro – *A euro*

L'**euro** est la devise de plusieurs pays d'Europe.
The **euro** is the currency of many European countries.

1745- Une phase – *A phase*

Ne porte pas attention à son style vestimentaire, ce n'est qu'**une phase**.
Don't pay attention to her clothing style, it's only **a phase**.

1746- La confusion – *Confusion*

Nous devions nous rencontrer à onze heures, mais il y a eu de la **confusion**.

We were supposed to meet at eleven o'clock, but there was some **confusion**.

1747- Une précision – *A precision*

Cette œuvre d'art a été sculptée avec **précision**.
This art piece was sculpted with **precision**.

1748- Une bombe – *A bomb*

Ils croyaient que ce passager avait caché **une bombe** dans le train.
They thought that this passenger had hidden **a bomb** on the train.

1749- Un bilan – *An assessment*

Il a complété **le bilan** de nos dépenses annuelles.
He has completed **the assessment** of our annual expenses.

1750- Immense – *Immense*

Nous nous sommes presque perdus dans sa maison, elle est **immense**!
We almost got lost is his house, it's **immense**!

1751- Massif|Massive – *Massive*

L'éléphant est le mammifère terrestre le plus **massif**.
The elephant is the most **massive** land mammal.

1752- Une chute – *A fall*

Elle s'est brisé le poignet à cause de **la chute**.
She broke her wrist because of **the fall**.

1753- Constant|Constante – *Constant*

Cette solitude **constante** va la rendre complètement folle.
This **constant** solitude is going to drive her completely crazy.

1754- Une compétence – *A competence*

Elle n'a pas les **compétences** requises pour accomplir ce travail.
She does not has the required **competencies** to accomplish this job.

1755- Intégrer – *To integrate*

Nous aimerions **intégrer** de nouvelles ressources cette année.
We would like **to integrate** new resources this year.

1756- Aérien|Aérienne – *Aerial*

Il a été arrêté par la patrouille **aérienne**.
He was arrested by the **aerial** patrol.

1757- Contrairement à – *Contrary to*

Contrairement à ce que tu crois, je n'ai rien fait de mal.
Contrary to what you believe, I have done nothing wrong.

1758- Une pierre – *A stone*

Sa maison est très robuste, car elle est faite en **pierre**.
His house is very sturdy, because it is made of **stone**.

1759- Socialiste – *Socialist*

Il est à la tête d'un mouvement **socialiste**.
He is at the head of a **socialist** movement.

1760- Sain|Saine – *Healthy*

C'est bien de faire de l'exercice, mais il te faut aussi une alimentation **saine**.
It's good to exercise, but you also need a **healthy** diet.

1761- Régulier|Régulière – *Regular*

Henry est un client **régulier**, il va au café chaque semaine.
Henry is a **regular** customer, he goes to the café every week.

1762- Une boîte – *A box*

As-tu besoin de plus de **boîtes** de déménagement?
Do you need more moving **boxes**?

1763- Financer – *To finance*

Mes parents ont accepté de **financer** mon voyage.
My parents have agreed **to finance** my trip.

1764- Une théorie – *A theory*

Pourrais-tu expliquer cette **théorie** à la classe?
Could you explain this **theory** to the class?

1765- Un hôtel – *A hotel*

Appelle-moi aussitôt que tu arrives à l'**hôtel**.
Call me as soon as you arrive to **the hotel**.

1766- Nier – *To deny*

Je sais qu'il est coupable, mais il a tout **nié**.
I know that he's guilty, but he **denied** everything.

1767- Un phénomène – *A phenomenon*

La photosynthèse est **un phénomène** naturel.
Photosynthesis is a natural **phenomenon**.

1768- Là-bas – *Over there*

Kelly est **là-bas**, elle nous attend.
Kelly is **over there**, she's waiting for us.

1769- Étonner – *To surprise/To amaze*

Tu vas voir, ce spectacle de cirque **étonnera** certainement tout le public.

You'll see, this circus show will certainly **amaze** the entire audience.

1770- La totalité – *The totality*

Vous devez prendre en compte **la totalité** des données.
You need to take into account **the totality** of the data.

1771- Un sort – *A curse*

Cette sorcière lui a jeté **un sort**!
This witch put **a curse** on him!

1772- Accéder – *To access*

Vous ne pouvez pas **accéder** à ces fichiers sans mon mot de passe.
You can't **access** these files withtout my password.

1773- Une église – *A church*

Cette **église** est en ruines, elle va bientôt être détruite.
This **church** is in ruins, it will soon be destroyed.

1774- Fortement – *Strongly*

Je vous recommande **fortement** d'être à l'heure.
I **strongly** advise you to be on time.

1775- Doter – *To provide*

J'aimerais **doter** ma classe d'un nouveau tableau blanc.
I would like **to provide** my class with a new whiteboard.

1776- Une contribution – *A contribution*

Nous lançons un nouveau projet, aimeriez-vous faire **une contribution**?
We're launching a new project, would you like to make **a contribution**?

1777- La profondeur – *The depth*

Plusieurs créatures inconnues se cachent dans les **profondeurs** de l'océan.
Many unknown creatures hide in the **depths** of the ocean.

1778- Émettre – *To issue*

Cet article a été **émis** par notre journaliste le plus talentueux.
This article was **issued** by our most talented journalist.

1779- Un test – *A test*

Nous vous ferons d'abord compléter une série de **tests**.
We will first make you complete a series of **tests**.

1780- Récupérer – *To get back*

Je te l'ai prêté il y a plus d'une semaine, j'aimerais le **récupérer**.
I lent it to you more than a week ago, I would like to **get** it **back**.

1781- La pêche – *Fishing/The peach*

Nous allons à **la pêche**, ensuite nous irons cueillir des **pêches**.
We are going **fishing**, then we will go pick some **peaches**.

1782- Une découverte – *A discovery*

Ce scientifique a fait **une découverte** importante.
This scientist has made an important **discovery**.

1783- Potentiel|Potentielle – *Potential*

Nous devons essayer d'impressionner ces clients **potentiels**.
We need to try to impress these **potential** clients.

1784- Agricole – *Agricultural*

Philippe étudie les sciences **agricoles** depuis trois ans.
Philippe has been studying **agricultural** sciences for three years.

1785- Intellectuel|Intellectuelle – *Intellectual*

Il s'agissait d'un cas sévère de déficience **intellectuelle**.
It was a severe case of **intellectual** disability.

1786- Une essence – *An essence/Gas*

L'augmentation du prix de l'**essence** est l'**essence** du problème.
The rising **gas** prices are **the essence** of the problem.

1787- Pencher – *To tilt*

Arrête de **pencher** l'armoire ou elle va tomber!
Stop **tilting** the cabinet or it will fall over!

1788- Un vice-président – *A vice-president*

Préparez-vous, **le vice-président** va déclarer une nouvelle importante.
Prepare yourselves, **the vide-president** is going to declare important news.

1789- Un coin – *A corner*

Tu aurais dû placer cette table dans **le coin** de la pièce.
You should have placed this table in **the corner** of the room.

1790- La tension – *Tension*

Il y a toujours eu de **la tension** entre nous.
There has always been **tension** between us.

1791- Un don – *A donation*

L'église acceptera votre **don** avec plaisir.
The church will gladly accept your **donation**.

1792- Un|Une artiste – *An artist*

Mélissa est **une artiste**, mais elle ne le sait pas encore.
Mélissa is **an artist**, but she doesn't know it yet.

1793- Fidèle – *Faithful*

Je sais qu'il est **fidèle**, je lui fais confiance.
I know that he's **faithful**, I trust him.

1794- Une grève – *A strike*

Les étudiants seront encore en **grève** pendant deux semaines.
The students are still going to be on **strike** for two weeks.

1795- Un achat – *A purchase*

Merci pour votre **achat**; votre article sera expédié d'ici trois jours.
Thank you for your **purchase**; your item will be shipped within three days.

1796- Mentionner – *To mention*

Vous avez oublié de **mentionner** que vous étiez enceinte.
You forgot **to mention** that you were pregnant.

1797- Une exécution – *An execution*

L'**exécution** du Roi a eu lieu sur la place publique.
The King's **execution** was held on the public square.

1798- Un uniforme – *A uniform*

Il est obligatoire de porter **un uniforme** à cette école.
It is compulsory to wear **a uniform** at this school.

1799- Exploiter – *To exploit*

Cette entreprise devrait avoir honte d'**exploiter** les travailleurs.
This company should be ashamed of **exploiting** the workers.

1800- Administratif|Administrative – *Administrative*

Notre bureau **administratif** est situé en Alberta.
Our **administrative** office is located in Alberta.

1801- Effectif|Effective – *Effective*

Cette mesure a été très **effective**, le projet avancera plus
rapidement.
This measure was very **effective**, the project will move forward
more rapidly.

1802- Communautaire – *Community*

Seriez-vous intéressé à participer à un projet **communautaire**?
Would you be interested in participating in a **community** project?

1803- Individuel|Individuelle – *Individual*

Chaque passager de l'avion a accès à un écran **individuel**.
Each passenger of the plane has access to an **individual** screen.

1804- Distinguer – *To distinguish*

Ils se ressemblent tellement, je n'arrive pas à les **distinguer** l'un de
l'autre.
They resemble each other so much, I can't **distinguish** them from
one another.

1805- Original|Originale – *Original*

Ces accessoires mode sont très **originaux**.
These fashion accessories are very **original**.

1806- Une surprise – *A surprise*

J'ai **une surprise** pour toi, suis-moi!
I have **a surprise** for you, follow me!

1807- Veiller – *To stay up/To look after*

Alphonse a **veillé** tard hier soir; il **veillait** sur sa mère malade.
Alphonse **stayed up** late last night; he was **looking after** his sick
mother.

1808- Une dette – *A debt*

Ce prisonnier a payé sa **dette** envers la société.
This prisoner has paid his **debt** to society.

1809- Une capitale – *A capital city*

La population est bien plus concentrée dans **la capitale**.
Population is much more concentrated in **the capital city**.

1810- Faciliter – *To facilitate*

Cette méthode va grandement **faciliter** la transition.
This method will highly **facilitate** the transition.

1811- Chanter – *To sing*

Apparemment, elle a une voix d'ange, mais je ne l'ai jamais entendue **chanter**.
Apparently, she has the voice of an angel, but I've never heard her **sing**.

1812- Une pension – *A pension*

Ces cotisations sont directement investies dans votre **pension**.
These contributions are directly invested in your **pension**.

1813- Une revue – *A magazine*

Ma grand-mère adore lire cette **revue** de cuisine.
My grandmother loves to read this cooking **magazine**.

1814- Clore – *To close*

Tout a été dit, nous pouvons **clore** le sujet.
Everything has been said, we can **close** the subject.

1815- La neige – *The snow*

Trente centimètres de **neige** sont attendus pour demain.

Thirty centimeters of **snow** are expected for tomorrow.

1816- Une figure – *A figure*

Même s'il n'est pas mon père, il est tout de même **une figure** paternelle.
Even if he's not my father, he is still a paternal **figure**.

1817- Une masse – *A mass*

Savez-vous comment calculer **la masse** d'un objet?
Do you know how to calculate **the mass** of an object?

1818- Le maintien – *The maintenance*

Nous visons **le maintien** de nos relations amicales avec la Chine.
We aim for **the maintenance** of our friendly relations with China.

1819- Étroit|Étroite – *Narrow*

Tu ne peux pas placer l'urne sur cette tablette, elle est trop **étroite**.
You can't place the urn on this shelf, it's too **narrow**.

1820- Un goût – *A taste*

Elle a **un goût** très développé pour le vin.
She has a very developed **taste** in wine.

1821- Une prestation – *A performance*

Toute la famille sera là pour assister à ta **prestation**.
The whole family will be there to attend your **performance**.

1822- Régner – *To reign*

Le Roi **régnait** sur un peuple désespéré.
The King **reigned** over a desperate people.

1823- Une catastrophe – *A catastrophe*

Nous nous dirigeons tout droit vers **une catastrophe**.

We are heading straight towards **a catastrophe**.

1824- Ressortir – *To go out again*

Je viens d'arriver et j'ai eu une longue journée, je n'ai pas envie de **ressortir**.

I just arrived and I had a long day, I don't feel like **going out again**.

1825- Susceptible – *Susceptible/Touchy*

Elle est **susceptible** de se mettre en colère; n'oublis pas qu'elle est très **susceptible**.

She is **susceptible** to becoming angry; don't forget that she's very **touchy**.

1826- Une manifestation – *A manifestation*

Cette action était **une manifestion** de courage.

This action was **a manifestation** of courage.

1827- Dormir – *To sleep*

Je suis épuisé, je dois aller **dormir**.

I'm exhausted, I need to go **to sleep**.

1828- Un lit – *A bed*

Son **lit** est gigantesque, il ne fera pas dans la pièce.

Her **bed** is gigantic, it won't fit in the room.

1829- Une bouche – *A mouth*

Ferme ta **bouche** quand tu manges, sinon c'est impoli.

Close your **mouth** when you eat, otherwise it's impolite.

1830- Une excuse – *An excuse*

Ce n'était qu'**une excuse** pour obtenir ce qu'elle voulait.

It was only **an excuse** to obtain what she wanted.

1831- La veille – *The day before*

Il s'est endormi dans l'autobus, car il n'avait pas beaucoup dormi **la veille**.

He fell asleep in the bus, because he hadn't slept much **the day before**.

1832- Content|Contente – *Glad*

Je suis **content** que vous appréciiez mon travail.

I'm **glad** you appreciate my work.

1833- Une exploitation – *An exploitation*

Ils veulent mettre fin à **l'exploitation** de cette ressource naturelle.

They want to end **the exploitation** of this natural resource.

1834- Triste – *Sad*

Je suis si **triste** que tu sois parti sans dire aurevoir.

I am so **sad** that you left without saying goodbye.

1835- Latin|Latine – *Latin*

Elle est la championne du monde en danse **latine**.

She's the world champion of **Latin** dance.

1836- Classique – *Classic*

Cette table de cuisine est élégante et **classique**.

This kitchen table is elegant and **classic**.

1837- Une alliance – *An alliance*

Ils ont formé **une alliance** en août deux mille seize.

They have formed **an alliance** in August two thousand sixteen.

1838- Une préoccupation – *A preoccupation*

Une certaine **préoccupation** l'empêchait d'avancer.

A certain **preoccupation** prevented her from moving forward.

1839- Une trace – *A trace*

Elle ne l'a jamais rappelé et elle a disparu sans laisser de **traces**.
She never called him back and she disappeared without a **trace**.

1840- Un logement – *A flat/An apartment*

J'ai visité le nouveau **logement** de Vincent; il est très petit.
I visited Vincent's new **apartment**; it's very small.

1841- Rassurer – *To reassure*

Il a tout fait pour la **rassurer**.
He did everything **to reassure** her.

1842- Une plainte – *A complaint*

J'ai demandé à parler au gérant, j'aimerais faire **une plainte**.
I asked to talk to the manager, I would like to make **a complaint**.

1843- Chaud|Chaude – *Warm/Hot*

L'eau de la piscine est trop **chaude**, je n'irai pas me baigner.
The water from the pool is too **warm**, I won't go swimming.

1844- Taire – *To keep quiet*

Arrête de parler, je t'ai demandé de te **taire**!
Stop talking, I asked you **to keep quiet**!

1845- Une émotion – *An emotion*

Cette relation est malsaine, il n'arrête pas de jouer avec ses **émotions**.
This relationship is unhealthy, he won't stop playing with her **emotions**.

1846- Judiciaire – *Judiciary*

J'ai confiance en leurs services **judiciaires**.

I trust their **judiciary** services.

1847- Progresser – *To progress*

Je n'arrive pas à me concentrer et ça m'empêche de **progresser**.
I can't concentrate and it's preventing me from **progressing**.

1848- Un langage – *A language*

L'amour est **un langage** universal.
Love is a universal **language**.

1849- Confronter – *To confront*

Elle a trop peur de **confronter** son agresseur en cour.
She's too afraid **to confront** her aggressor in court.

1850- Strict|Stricte – *Strict*

La loi est très **stricte** en ce qui a trait à ce genre de crime.
The law is very **strict** in what has to do with this type of crime.

1851- Un club – *A club*

Yvonne fait partie d'**un club** de lecture.
Yvonne is part of a book **club**.

1852- Ouvrier|Ouvrière – *Worker*

Les conditions de travail des **ouvriers** se sont améliorées.
The **workers'** working conditions have improved.

1853- La souffrance – *Suffering*

Une nouvelle présence dans la maison pourrait apaiser ta **souffrance**.
A new presence in the house could ease your **suffering**.

1854- Une observation – *An observation*

Permettez-moi de partager mes **observations**.
Allow me to share my **observations**.

1855- Rétablir – *To re-establish*

Cette loi sera **réétablie** le premier avril.
This law will be **re-established** on the first of April.

1856- Un secours – *A rescue*

Il allait se noyer, mais le sauveteur est venu à son **secours**!
He was going to drown, but the lifeguard came to his **rescue**!

1857- Une passion – *A passion*

Il n'y a aucun doute que la musique soit sa **passion**.
There is no doubt that music is his **passion**.

1858- Une rupture – *A break-up*

Je ne sais pas comment l'aider à oublier sa **rupture** avec Émile.
I don't know how to help her forget about her **break-up** with Émile.

1859- Un Office – *An Office*

Ce terme n'est pas accepté par **l'Office** de la langue française.
This term is not accepted by **the Office** de la langue française.

1860- Compliquer – *To complicate*

Elle a un talent pour toujours **compliquer** les choses.
She has a talent for always **complicating** things.

1861- Assumer – *To assume*

Elle ne m'a pas appelé, alors j'**assume** qu'elle ne viendrait pas.
She didn't call me, so I'm **assuming** that she won't come.

1862- Éprouver – *To feel*

Je n'avais jamais **éprouvé** autant de tristesse.
I had never **felt** so much sadness.

1863- Un immeuble – *A building*

Cet **immeuble** va être rénové l'an prochain.
This **building** is going to be renovated next year.

1864- Un rendez-vous – *An appointment/A date*

J'ai **un rendez-vous** avec Danièle ce soir; j'irai la rejoindre au
restaurant après mon **rendez-vous** chez le dentiste.
I have **a date** with Danièle this evening; I will meet her at the
restaurant after my dentist **appointment**.

1865- Un argument – *An argument*

Son **argument** est invalide, car il n'a aucune preuve.
His **argument** is invalid, because he has no proof.

1866- Une planète – *A planet*

Il y a une haute concentration de mercure sur cette **planète**.
There is a high concentration of mercury on this **planet**.

1867- Partiel|Partielle – *Partial*

Ils ont seulement trouvé une empreinte de pouce **partielle**.
Theey only found a **partial** thumb print.

1868- Délicat|Délicate – *Delicate*

Cette fleur est colorée et si **délicate**.
This flower is colorful and so **delicate**.

1869- Un attentat – *An attack*

Nous aimerions pouvoir oublier cet **attentat** terroriste.
We would like to be able to forget this terrorist **attack**.

1870- Boire – *To drink*

Bois beaucoup d'eau, tu te sentiras mieux.
Drink a lot of water, you'll feel better.

1871- La richesse – *The richness*

Connaître deux langues permet **une richesse** culturelle plus développée.
Knowing two languages allows for a more developed cultural **richness**.

1872- Une caisse – *A register*

Il a pointé son arme sur moi et a exigé que je vide **la caisse**.
He pointed his weapon on me and demanded that I emptied **the register**.

1873- Le hasard – *Chance*

Par **hasard**, connaîtrais-tu le numéro de Sophie?
By any **chance**, would you happen to know Sophie's number?

1874- Un héros – *A hero*

Mon père a toujours été mon **héros**.
My father has always been my **hero**.

1875- Le maire – *The mayor*

Le maire sera présent à cet événement.
The mayor will be present at this event.

1876- Un incident – *An incident*

Ce n'était qu'un petit **incident**, tout ira bien.
It was only a little **incident**, everything will be fine.

1877- Un café – *A coffee/A café*

Nous allons à ce **café** tous les jours; leur **café** est délicieux.
We go to this **café** everyday; their **coffee** is delicious.

1878- Une annonce – *An announcement*

Ils ont tous été choqués par cette **annonce**.
They were all shocked by this **announcement**.

1879- Régulièrement – *Regularly*

Tu dois faire de l'exercice **régulièrement** pour être en bonne santé.
You must exercise **regularly** to be in good health.

1880- Une oreille – *An ear*

La musique est trop forte, j'ai mal aux **oreilles**.
The music is too loud, my **ears** hurt.

1881- Foutre – *To shove off*

Tu as bien fait de dire à ce pervers d'aller se faire **foutre**.
You were right to tell this pervert to **shove off**.

1882- Apercevoir – *To see*

On peut **apercevoir** le sommet des montagnes d'ici.
We can **see** the top of the mountains from here.

1883- Refléter – *To reflect*

Ce projet doit **refléter** vos valeurs personnelles.
This project must **reflect** your personal values.

1884- Bouger – *To move*

Elle était terrifiée et incapable de **bouger**.
She was terrified and unable to **move**.

1885- Une foule – *A crowd*

Je ne t'ai pas vue dans **la foule**, où étais-tu?
I didn't see you in **the crowd**, where were you?

1886- Chrétien|Chrétienne – *Christian*

Toute sa famille est **chrétienne**.
His whole family is **Christian**.

1887- Isoler – *To isolate*

Il a choisi de s'**isoler** pour écrire son livre en paix.
He chose to **isolate** himself to write his book in peace.

1888- Un pont – *A bridge*

Il y a beaucoup de trafic sur **le pont** à cette heure-ci.
There is a lot of traffic on **the bridge** at this hour.

1889- Une égalité – *Equality*

Les femmes continuent à se battre pour **l'égalité**.
Women continue to fight for **equality**.

1890- Une tenue – *An outfit*

Sa **tenue** est à la fois classique et audacieuse.
Her **outfit** is both classic and bold.

1891- Animer – *To liven up*

Il ne savait pas comment **animer** la foule.
He didn't know how **to liven up** the crowd.

1892- Une norme – *A norm*

Maryse est simplement une exception à la **norme**.
Maryse is simply an exception to the **norm**.

1893- Une piste – *A trail*

Je connais une très bonne **piste** pour faire du vélo.
I know a very good **trail** for cycling.

1894- Préserver – *To preserve*

Ce qui est le plus important pour lui, c'est de **préserver** sa réputation.
What's most important to him is **to preserve** his reputation.

1895- Un hommage – *A tribute*

Cette chanson est **un hommage** à sa grand-mère.
This song is **a tribute** to his grandmother.

1896- Inférieur|Inférieure – *Inferior*

Tu n'as aucune raison de te sentir **inférieur**.
You have no reason to feel **inferior**.

1897- Un match – *A game*

Nous avons perdu **le match** le plus important de la saison.
We lost the most important **game** of the season.

1898- Une statistique – *Statistics*

Selon les **statistiques**, ça devrait fonctionner.
According to the **statistics**, it should work.

1899- Gouvernemental|Gouvernementale – *Governmental*

Certaines responsabilités **gouvernementales** n'ont pas été respectées.

Certain **governmental** responsibilities have not been respected.

1900- Exécuter – *To carry out*

Cette tâche a été **exécutée** à la perfection.
This task has been **carried out** to perfection.

1901- Une tragédie – *A tragedy*

La mort de cet auteur est une véritable **tragédie**.
The death of this author is a real **tragedy**.

1902- La distribution – *Distribution*

Nous sommes spécialisés dans **la distribution** de nourriture.
We are specialized in food **distribution**.

1903- Un scandale – *A scandal*

Son changement de sexe a causé **un scandale**.
His sex change caused **a scandal**.

1904- La pointe – *The tip*

Il croyait avoir tout vu, mais ce n'était que **la pointe** de l'iceberg.
He thought he had seen it all, but it was only **the tip** of the iceberg.

1905- Chinois|Chinoise – *Chinese*

Normand a toujours mal au ventre après avoir mangé des mets **chinois**.
Normand always has a stomach ache after eating **Chinese** food.

1906- Un bénéfice – *A benefit*

Elle a eu une voiture neuve pour son anniversaire; c'est **le bénéfice** d'avoir des parents riches.
She got a new car for her birthday; that's **the benefit** of having rich parents.

1907- Un billet – *A ticket*

Nous partons pour le concert dans cinq minutes, n'oublis pas ton **billet**!

We leave for the concert in five minutes, don't forget your **ticket**!

1908- Un choc – *A shock*

Je ne pouvais pas y croire; c'était un **choc**.

I could not believe it; it was a **shock**.

1909- Une proportion – *A proportion*

Les **proportions** ne sont pas assez équilibrées dans cette recette.

The **proportions** are not balanced enough in this recipe.

1910- Irakien|Irakienne – *Iraqi*

Elle a épousé un ancien soldat **irakien**.

She married a former **Iraqi** soldier.

1911- Briser – *To break*

Nicolas est un véritable idiot; il a **brisé** le coeur de Noémie.

Nicolas is a true idiot; he **broke** Noémie's heart.

1912- La destruction – *Destruction*

La guerre n'est que violence et **destruction**.

War is nothing but violence and **destruction**.

1913- Reculer – *To back up*

Vous êtes trop près du bord, **reculez** un peu.

You're too close to the edge, **back up** a little.

1914- Un critère – *A standard*

Vos aptitudes ne répondent pas à nos **critères**.

Your aptitudes do not meet our **standards**.

1915- Gardien|Gardienne – *Guard/Guardian*

Le voleur a attaqué **le gardien** de sécurité.
The robber attacked the security **guard**.

1916- Une adresse – *An address*

Donne-moi ton **adresse**, je vais venir te chercher à six heures.
Give me your **address**, I will come get you at six o'clock.

1917- Un canal – *A channel*

L'eau se rend aux tuyaux en traversant ce **canal**.
The water reaches the pipes by going through this **channel**.

1918- Conservateur|Conservatrice – *Conservative*

Je ne suis pas d'accord avec cette politique **conservatrice**.
I do not agree with this **conservative** policy.

1919- Transporter – *To carry*

Tu es lourde, je ne pourrai pas te **transporter** toute la journée.
You're heavy, I won't be able **to carry** you all day.

1920- Brûler – *To burn*

Certains trouvent qu'il est apaisant de regarder un feu **brûler**.
Some find it relaxing to watch a fire **burn**.

1921- Une manœuvre – *A manoeuvre*

Elle a dû effectuer **une manœuvre** pour éviter le cerf sur la route.
She had to perform **a manoeuvre** to avoid the deer on the road.

1922- La monnaie – *The change*

Merci, vous pouvez garder **la monnaie**.
Thank you, you can keep **the change**.

1923- La réception – *The reception/The front desk*

Vous pouvez rejoindre **la réception** en tout temps.
You may reach **the front desk** at all times.

1924- Quelconque – *Any*

Ce n'est pas qu'un chien **quelconque**, c'est mon meilleur ami.
It's not just **any** dog, it's my best friend.

1925- Le courrier – *The mail*

Peux-tu vérifier **le courrier** avant de partir?
Can you check **the mail** before you leave?

1926- Grandir – *To grow*

Tu as tellement **grandi** depuis la dernière fois que je t'ai vu.
You've **grown** so much since the last time I saw you.

1927- Élaborer – *To elaborate*

Nous devons **élaborer** un plan astucieux.
We must **elaborate** a clever plan.

1928- Un doigt – *A finger*

Il n'a pas levé **le doigt** pour l'aider.
He did not lift **a finger** to help her.

1929- Illustrer – *To illustrate*

Cette métaphore **illustre** parfaitement ma pensée.
This metaphor **illustrates** my thoughts perfectly.

1930- Une poche – *A pocket*

N'oublis pas que mes clés sont dans tes **poches**.
Don't forget that my keys are in your **pockets**.

1931- La transmission – *Transmission*

La transmission de tous les fichiers est complétée.
Transmission of all the files is completed.

1932- Éclater – *To burst*

Si tu n'arrêtes pas de souffler, le ballon va **éclater**.
If you don't stop blowing, the balloon will **burst**.

1933- La honte – *The shame*

La honte qu'il ressent est sa punition.
The shame he feels is his punishment.

1934- Une faiblesse – *A weakness*

Comment savais-tu que c'était ma plus grande **faiblesse**?
How did you know it was my biggest **weakness**?

1935- Une fédération – *A federation*

Ces États forment **une fédération**.
These States form **a federation**.

1936- Presser – *To squeeze*

J'ai **pressé** vingt citrons pour faire ce jus.
I have **squeezed** twenty lemons to make this juice.

1937- Affronter – *To face*

Aujourd'hui, tu devras **affronter** tes peurs.
Today, you will have **to face** your fears.

1938- Le bonheur – *Happiness*

Le bonheur ne s'achète pas.
Happiness cannot be bought.

1939- Formuler – *To formulate*

Je ne sais pas comment **formuler** ma question.
I don't know how **to formulate** my question.

1940- Crier – *To shout*

J'ai entendu les voisins **crier** toute la nuit.
I heard the neighbors **shout** all night.

1941- La pauvreté – *Poverty*

Cette organisation vise à réduire **la pauvreté**.
This organization aims to reduce **poverty**.

1942- Un bâtiment – *A building*

Ce **bâtiment** est vide depuis des années.
This **building** has been empty for years.

1943- Époux|Épouse – *Spouse*

Je te présenterai Nathalie, mon **épouse**.
I'll introduce you to Nathalie, my **spouse**.

1944- Se mêler – *To meddle*

Je ne veux pas **me mêler** de ce qui ne me regarde pas.
I don't want **to meddle** with what doesn't concern me.

1945- Une firme – *A firm*

Grégoire est le président d'**une firme** réputée.
Grégoire is the president of a renown **firm**.

1946- Élargir – *To widen*

L'ouverture est trop étroite; nous allons devoir l'**élargir**.
The opening is too narrow; we will need to **widen** it.

1947- Électeur|Électrice – *Elector*

Les **électeurs** ont voté.
The **electors** have voted.

1948- Plonger – *To dive*

Tu as perdu la tête si tu crois que je vais **plonger** dans cette eau sale.
You've lost your mind if you think I'm going **to dive** in this dirty water.

1949- Un véhicule – *A vehicle*

Veuillez sortir du **véhicule**.
Please step out of **the vehicle**.

1950- Fuir – *To flee*

Il est trop orgueilleux pour **fuir**.
He is too proud to **flee**.

1951- Chercheur|Chercheuse – *Researcher*

Les **chercheurs** viennent de découvrir cette nouvelle espèce.
The **researchers** have just discovered this new species.

1952- Un médicament – *Medication*

Je dois prendre mes **médicaments** avant de me coucher.
I must take my **medication** before I go to sleep.

1953- Une personnalité – *A personality*

Cette femme a une merveilleuse **personnalité**.
This woman has a wonderful **personality**.

1954- Inventer – *To invent*

Ce scientist a **inventé** une nouvelle machine.
This scientist has **invented** a new machine.

1955- Principalement – *Mainly*

Nous faisons ceci **principalement** pour t'aider.
We are doing this **mainly** to help you.

1956- La prudence – *Caution*

N'oublis pas ton casque : **la prudence** d'abord!
Don't forget your helmet: **caution** first!

1957- Un stade – *A stadium*

Ce concert aura lieu dans **un stade** de football.
This concert will be held in a football **stadium**.

1958- Une liaison – *A connection*

Ne tentez pas de faire **la liaison** électrique par vous-même.
Do not attempt to make the electrical **connection** by yourself.

1959- Varier – *To vary*

La couleur réelle peut **varier** de ce que vous voyez à l'écran.
The real color can **vary** from what you see on the screen.

1960- Québécois|Québécoise – *From Quebec/In Quebec*

La Saint-Jean-Baptiste est la fête nationale **québécoise**.
Saint-Jean-Baptist Day is national holiday **in Quebec**.

1961- Ordonner – *To order*

Je t'**ordonne** d'aller dans ta chambre!
I **order** you to go in your room!

1962- Bonjour – *Hi*

Bonjour, comment allez-vous aujourd'hui?
Hi, how are you today?

1963- Une morale – *A moral*

Explique-moi **la morale** de cette histoire.
Explain **the moral** of this story to me.

1964- Contester – *To contest*

Contester l'autorité ne va te mener nulle part.
Contesting authority won't get you anywhere.

1965- Nécessairement – *Necessarily*

Il a applaudi, mais ça ne veut pas **nécessairement** dire qu'il a écouté.
He applauded, but that doesn't **necessarily** mean that he listened.

1966- La détermination – *Determination*

Il peut accomplir n'importe quoi avec une telle **détermination**.
He can accomplish anything with such **determination**.

1967- Un congrès – *A congress*

Mon mari est en Californie pour **un congrès**.
My husband is in California for **a congress**.

1968- Semblable – *Similar*

Cette robe est **semblable** à celle que ta mère m'a achetée.
This dress is **similar** to the one your mother bought for me.

1969- Préoccuper – *To concern*

Cette situation nous **préoccupe** tous.
This situation **concerns** all of us.

1970- Un dépôt – *A deposit*

Vous devez d'abord faire **un dépôt** de soixante dollars.
You must first make **a deposit** of sixty dollars.

1971- Une consultation – *A consultation*

Toutes les **consultations** sont gratuites à la clinique.
All **consultations** are free at the clinic.

1972- Multiplier – *To multiply*

Les fourmis n'arrêtent pas de se **multiplier**, appelle l'exterminateur.
The ants won't stop **multiplying**, call the exterminator.

1973- Une dame – *A lady*

Cette **dame** a demandé à voir le gérant.
This **lady** has asked to see the manager.

1974- La joie – *Joy*

Cette rencontre m'a apporté beaucoup de **joie**.
This meeting has brought me a lot of **joy**.

1975- Durable – *Durable*

Cette échelle est **durable**, car elle est faite en acier.
This ladder is **durable**, because it is made of steel.

1976- La faim – *Hunger*

Ce pays est dévasté par **la faim** et la pauvreté.
This country is devastated by **hunger** and poverty.

1977- Une considération – *A consideration*

Votre **considération** a beaucoup d'importance pour moi; je vous admire.
Your **consideration** has a lot of importance to me; I admire you.

1978- Recommander – *To recommend*

Faites-le si vous le voulez, mais je ne le **recommande** pas.

Do it if you want, but I don't **recommend** it.

1979- Un concept – *A concept*

Ce nouveau **concept** attire l'attention des médias.
This new **concept** is drawing the media's attention.

1980- Le cerveau – *The brain*

L'aire visuelle du **cerveau** est à l'arrière.
The visual area of **the brain** is in the back.

1981- Un truc – *A trick*

J'ai entendu dire que ce magicien avait un nouveau **truc**.
I heard that this magician had a new **trick**.

1982- Allié|Alliée – *Ally*

L'Angleterre était leur **alliée** en temps de guerre.
England was their **ally** in wartime.

1983- Excuser – *To excuse*

Excusez-moi, il est tard et je dois partir.
Excuse me, it's late and I have to leave.

1984- Arabe – *Arabic/Arab*

J'aimerais apprendre comment écrire l'**arabe**.
I would like to learn how to write in **Arabic**.

1985- Diffuser – *To disseminate*

Il est maintenant plus facile que jamais de **diffuser** des informations.
It is now easier than ever **to disseminate** information.

1986- Budgétaire – *Budgetary*

Cette décision aura un impact **budgétaire** considérable.
This decision will have a considerable **budgetary** impact.

1987- Inquiétant|Inquiétante – *Worrying*

Nos profits sont plus bas que prévu; ces chiffres sont **inquiétants**.
Our profit is lower than expected; these numbers are **worrying**.

1988- Inclure – *To include*

Cet ensemble **inclut** une table et quatre chaises.
This set **includes** one table and four chairs.

1989- Scolaire – *Academic*

Ta réussite **scolaire** est ce qui importe le plus.
Your **academic** success is what matters the most.

1990- Un style – *A style*

Elle a **un style** très particulier; elle sait se faire remarquer.
She has a very particular **style**; she knows how to get noticed.

1991- Combler – *To fill*

Malheureusement, ce poste a déjà été **comblé**.
Unfortunately, this position has already been **filled**.

1992- Annuler – *To cancel*

Cliquez ici pour **annuler** votre commande.
Click here to **cancel** your order.

1993- Joueur|Joueuse – *Player*

Les **joueurs** iront célébrer leur victoire après le match.
The **players** will go celebrate their victory after the game.

1994- Bloquer – *To block*

La crème solaire **bloque** les rayons ultraviolets.
Sunscreen **blocks** ultraviolet rays.

1995- Une interprétation – *An interpretation*

Son **interprétation** est différente de la mienne.
His **interpretation** is different than mine.

1996- Une ombre – *A shadow*

J'ai cru voir **une ombre** bouger dans le coin de la pièce.
I thought I saw **a shadow** move in the corner of the room.

1997- Un séjour – *A stay*

Bienvenue à notre hôtel, nous espérons que vous apprécierez votre **séjour**.
Welcome to our hotel, we hope that you'll enjoy your **stay**.

1998- Guider – *To guide*

Nous avons laissé la mer nous **guider** jusqu'à cette île.
We let the sea **guide** us to this island.

1999- Spécialiser – *To specialize*

Il a décidé de se **spécialiser** dans la neurochirurgie.
He has decided **to specialize** in neurosurgery.

2000- Bien – *Good*

Je vais **bien** aujourd'hui, comment vas-tu?
I'm **good** today, how are you?

MORE FROM LINGO MASTERY

**Do you know what the hardest
thing for a French learner is?**

Finding PROPER reading material that
they can handle...which is precisely the
reason we've written this book!

Teachers love giving out tough, expert-level literature to their
students, books that present many new problems to the reader
and force them to search for words in a dictionary every five
minutes — it's not entertaining, useful or motivating for the
student at all, and many soon give up on learning at all!

In this book we have compiled 20 easy-to-read, compelling and
fun stories that will allow you to expand your vocabulary and
give you the tools to improve your grasp of the wonderful French
tongue.

How French Short Stories for Beginners works:

- Each story will involve an important lesson of the tools in the French language (Verbs, Adjectives, Past Tense, Giving Directions, and more), involving an interesting and entertaining story with realistic dialogues and day-to-day situations.

- The summaries follow a synopsis in French and in English of what you just read, both to review the lesson and for you to see if you understood what the tale was about.

- At the end of those summaries, you'll be provided with a list of the most relevant vocabulary involved in the lesson, as well as slang and sayings that you may not have understood at first glance!

- Finally, you'll be provided with a set of tricky questions in French, providing you with the chance to prove that you learned something in the story. Don't worry if you don't know the answer to any — we will provide them immediately after, but no cheating!

So look no further! Pick up your copy of **French Short Stories for Beginners** and start learning French right now!

FREE BOOK REVEALS THE 6 STEP BLUEPRINT THAT TOOK STUDENTS **FROM LANGUAGE LEARNERS TO FLUENT IN 3 MONTHS**

- **6 Unbelievable Hacks** that will accelerate your learning curve
- **Mind Training:** why memorizing vocabulary is easy
- **One Hack To Rule Them All:** This <u>secret nugget</u> will blow you away...

Head over to <u>LingoMastery.com/hacks</u>
and claim your free book now!

CONCLUSION

You made it!

After going through this list of the **2000 Most Common Words in French**, you are now fully equipped to take your learning of the French language to a whole new level. As we mentioned earlier, understanding the meaning of these words is a great first step in learning the language, but you will also need to *practice* using them in different situations to truly acquire their meaning. It's true: conversation and writing are the best ways to familiarize yourself with new vocabulary, and maybe even discover some new ways to use the words or some less common meanings that were not presented in this book. And remember: once you've studied them thoroughly, these words should help you develop your understanding of non-fiction to 84%, your understanding of fiction to 86.1%, and your oral speech to 92.7%. Just imagine what you could do with all that knowledge!

As you were reading this book, you probably noticed how similar French can be to English. Indeed, many words – pronounciation aside – are exactly the same! The only tricky part remains to distinguish the masculine from the feminine, which will come naturally to you after some time and a lot of practice.

I am happy to have helped you with your practice of French and hope to see you again soon; we'll surely meet again in future books and learning material.

So take care and study hard, and don't forget the 4 tips we gave you at the beginning if you want to become a pro of the French language:

1. Practice hard!
2. Don't limit yourself to these 2000 words!
3. Grab a study partner!
4. Write a story!

With everything covered in what has to do with the most common vocabulary words, you are now free to use that knowledge to learn even more French, such as grammar and punctuation rules. Mastering French will be quite a journey, but rejoice: you're already more than halfway there!

If you liked the book, we would also really appreciate a little review wherever you bought it.

THANKS FOR READING!